The History
and Politics
of Private Prisons

The History
and Politics
of Private Prisons

A Comparative Analysis

Martin P. Sellers

Rutherford • Madison • Teaneck
Fairleigh Dickinson University Press
London and Toronto: Associated University Presses

Associated University Presses
440 Forsgate Drive
Cranbury, NJ 08512

Associated University Presses
25 Sicilian Avenue
London WC1A 2QH, England

Associated University Presses
P.O. Box 338, Port Credit
Mississauga, Ontario,
L5G 4L8 Canada

The paper used in this publication meets the requirements
of the American National Standard for Permanence of Paper
for Printed Library Materials Z39.48-1984.

Library of Congress Cataloging-in-Publication Data

Sellers, Martin P.
    The history and politics of private prisons: a comparative analysis /
Martin P. Sellers.
        p.   cm.
    Includes bibliographical references and index.
    ISBN 0-8386-3492-3 (alk. paper)
    1. Prisons—United States—History.   2. Privatization—United States
History.   I. Title.
HV9466.S45   1993
365′.973—dc20   91-59054
                                                                          CIP

PRINTED IN THE UNITED STATES OF AMERICA

Contents

List of Illustrations

Tables

LIST OF ILLUSTRATIONS

Figures

Acknowledgments

I am grateful to my wife Patricia and our children, Christina, Brian, Jacqueline, Martin, and Madeline, for the opportunity costs they paid and the sacrifices made while I worked. I appreciate the help and support I received from many others including Dr. Daryl Fair of Trenton State College, Dr. Harry Bailey of Temple University, Dr. Jim Abrahamson of Campbell University, and the staff of the Department of Government and History at Campbell. My appreciation also goes out to the C. Rich Library at Campbell University and the reference personnel there.

The History
and Politics
of Private Prisons

1

Privatization: Overview

The privatization of public services is a matter of interest to private and public sector managers, analysts, and theorists. There is interest on the part of both proponents and opponents of privatization in both sectors for determining the impact and cost of privatization on service providers and suppliers.

In the corrections industry a handful of private companies believe that economic profits exist in the production of correctional services, not just in contracting of specific services but in the production of the entire array of services available to a prison population; i.e., contracting for the management of entire facilities including all services and programs provided therein. Perhaps the strongest argument in favor of private contracting of prisons is the presumption that contracting would be similar in success or failure to the private contracting of other public services (Logan, 1985). Although not all contracted services have been more efficiently or effectively provided by the private sector, Emanuel S. Savas, Harry P. Hatry, Robert W. Poole, and others have found a wide range of public services that have proven to be more efficiently provided by the private sector (Savas 1982; Hatry 1983; Poole 1980). If correction services can be as efficiently produced by the private sector with no discernible difference in the level of services, then pitfalls associated with public sector production of prison services (discussed in chapter 3) can be avoided. Competition would be free to effectuate cost reductions, and implicit costs attributable to public production could be circumvented.

The intent of this study is to provide some insight into the privatization of prisons and to test hypotheses that suggest that privatization of prisons is beneficial to the public, especially the argument that private prisons are managed more efficiently. But why is there such a strong appeal for having the private sector provide goods and services that the public sector is now providing? According to economic theory, the market system, by depending upon the rationing function of prices and the self-interest of competition, efficiently allocates scarce resources so that society can maximize satisfaction

(McConnell 1987). In other words, consumers, through purchases based upon competitively derived prices, determine the ultimate mix of goods and services that will be produced from scarce resources.

Society has come to depend upon private industry to advance this country's economic position by relying on competition to induce innovation, research, technological change, and managerial and entrepreneurial advances. Society has appealed to the ideal of self-interest, which assumes that when every individual pursues his own interests, society will improve and advance. This implies the efficient allocation of resources (that is, resources allocated according to the needs of society) and the equitable distribution of income that comes as a result of competition sustained by open and free movement of buyers and sellers in and out of markets. The view presented in this study is that public sector production of goods and services (specifically, prisons) does not benefit from the ideal of economic self-interest.

Thomas Jefferson believed that a large and complicated public administration is not necessary or desirable. He believed that private enterprise manages much better than government all concerns to which it is equal. Jefferson stated,

> Having always observed that public works are always much less advantageously managed than the same are by private hands, I have thought it better for the public to go to the market for whatever it wants which is found there, for there competition brings it down to the minimum value. (Caldwell 1944, 161)

All governments are searching for ways to reduce spending. Since the 1970s, the Thatcher, and now the Major, administrations in Britain have been successful in returning much of the nationalized industries back to ownership by the public through sale of stocks to large investment groups, wealthy families, employees, and unions.

In the United States, the Reagan administration's 1980 campaign platform was floored with planks calling for government efficiency, reduced government, less regulation, decreased provision of services, oversight rather than over-provision, as well as other conservative goals. Despite this, the national budget had never been so gigantic, nor had government spending ever been as high a proportion of the GNP as it was during the Reagan years, and is now during Bush's tenure in the White House (see table 1.1).[1]

With spending continuing to rise and total tax revenues steadily increasing, the call from the public has been to hold down government spending, decrease the role of federal intervention, decrease taxes, increase the role of volunteers, and increase private sector's responsibility for producing services (see table 1.2).[2] The federal government responded by providing states with less: Federal grant dollars to the states have been on the decline since the Reagan era. High federal taxes have gone toward transfer payments and defense (see table 1.3).

Table 1.1
Government Spending as a Percent of GNP

Fiscal Year	Federal Government Spending	Total Government Expenditures
1980	22.1%	30.7%
1981	22.7%	31.0%
1982	23.8%	32.4%
1983	24.3%	33.0%
1984	23.1%	31.4%
1985	23.9%	32.4%
1986	23.7%	32.3%
1987	22.7%	31.9%
1988	22.3%	31.5%
1989	22.3%	31.6%
1990	23.2%	32.7%

Source: Complied from Fiscal Year 1992 Budget of the United States Government, Historical Tables, p.180.

Table 1.2
Tax Revenues (Billions)

Fiscal Year	Federal Tax Revenues	All Tax Revenues
1980	517.1	772.1
1981	599.3	880.7
1982	617.8	923.4
1983	600.6	930.5
1984	666.5	1037.0
1985	734.1	1131.2
1986	769.1	1194.6
1987	854.1	1313.6
1988	909.0	1397.8
1989	990.7	1516.6
1990	749.7	1586.8

Compiled from Fiscal Year 1992, Budget of the United States Government, Historical Tables, p.178. What seems to be discrepancies between table 1.1 percentge for spending and table 1.2 figures for revenues between Federal and all governments may be explained in part by the fact that the Federal government takes advantage of deficit spending.

Table 1.3
Grants-in-Aid
(In Constant FY 1982 Dollars)
in Billions of Dollars

As a Percent of Federal Outlays

Years	Percent
1980	15.5%
1981	14.0
1982	11.8
1983	11.4
1984	11.5
1985	11.2
1986	11.3
1987	10.8
1988	10.8
1989	10.7
1990	10.9

Source: Historical Tables, *Budget of the United States Government*, Fiscal Year 1992, U.S. Government Printing Office, 1991, p. 132; and Sellers, Martin P. "Privatization of Urban Services In North Carolina," *Privatization Review* (Summer 1990); 51–64.

"A key constructive alternative to solve the problems that are overtaking our society is *privatization*" [emphasis added] (Linowes, 1989, 3). An important terminology clarification regarding producing goods and services must be made here. As Ted Kolderie states in his article on privatization concepts, provision of a service is a policy decision and production of a service is an administrative action (Kolderie 1986, 285). That is, government can be responsible for ensuring the ongoing existence of a service by creating laws for its control, maintenance, and funding and yet allow the service to be "produced" in the private sector. Most proponents of the privatization of prisons are pressing for the production of prison services (management of entire facilities) to be shared with the private sector and the responsibility for provision of prison services to remain with the government. This research follows Ted Kolderie's distinction between service provision and production.

Privatization has been an ongoing theme supported by the Reagan and Bush administrations. During his first year of office, Reagan created and commissioned the President's Private Sector Survey on Cost Control (PPSSCC). Heading the Commission was Peter Grace, Chairman and Executive Officer of W. R. Grace Corporation. The goal of the "Grace Commission" was to determine which government services could be better and more efficiently produced by the private sector, and to determine the feasibility of the privatization of a host of services. Privatization was defined by the Grace Commission as "the transfer of the production of goods and services from the public sector to the private sector of the economy."[3] Chapter 2 provides a detailed discussion on the meaning of privatization of public services.

James M. Buchanan and Emanuel S. Savas have developed different models for determining which public services lend themselves to privatization. Buchanan's model fosters a priori arguments based upon the "degree of publicness" a good or service engenders (Buchanan 1968, 173–75). Two variables inherent in the Buchanan model are (1) the degree of indivisibility of a service and (2) the size of the interacting group. The Emanuel S. Savas model includes four characteristics (variables) that he uses to identify the nature of goods and services and to locate them somewhere on a continuum between collectively consumable or individually consumable goods and the ability of the purchase of these goods to be controlled by price as in what Savas calls toll goods and common pool goods. Both models convey the idea that some goods and services can be more efficiently and effectively produced by the private sector.

The intention of this study is to build on these models' assumption that prisons render a service that can be measured in dollars and that can be competed for in the private sector. If this is so, a private company should be able to produce the same scope, level, and consistency of services (or an increased level of services) at the same cost or less when compared to the public sector because the latter does not compete for prison management contracts while private sector companies would.

Private prisons are not only claimed by some to be more efficient economically, but are in political debate as well. Current literature and models present only limited political perspectives, however, and fail to analyze aspects of the privatization of prisons that would prove useful to political officials, administrators, legislators, and political scientists who attempt to make substantive judgments based on empirical evidence. The overall goal of this study is to determine if privatization of prisons continues to be feasible and beneficial and whether prison management should be shifted to the private sector. If this is so, government could meet the growing demand for better and more plentiful incarceration facilities at a lower cost to the public. Because of the somewhat limited amount of research information available on the privatization of corrections, neither government nor private industry has collected enough evidence of historical data to determine whether privatization of prisons is a viable strategy. As Charles Logan writes in his article on prisons and competition,

> It is one thing to believe that only the state has the right to imprison someone. It is another matter entirely to believe that only the state can run a prison in a fair, humane, effective and economical fashion. The first belief is a matter of political philosophy; the second is an empirical proposition. (Logan 1985, 469)

Goals

The specific goals of this study were to determine whether:

(1) given the same level and scope of services, private sector companies can produce the needed cell space and manage correction facilities at the same or lower cost than the public sector;

(2) private sector prison facilities are more efficiently run than public sector prisons at a comparable level of services;

(3) barriers other than costs are inhibiting the growth of the private sector prison system;

(4) public prison officials believe that a wider scope and variety of barriers to privatization exist than is actually the case;

(5) and to determine what real barriers exist and how to overcome them.

The first goal regarding costs requires examination of public and private facility budgets, an analysis of the programs and program service levels, and a comparison of expenditures through a cost-efficiency analysis (Williams and Anderson 1975; Hatry 1979). The intent here is to determine if private sector prisons can save tax dollars and still provide the same level of services. The remaining goals seek to determine what barriers to entry into the private prison market exist and how many of these barriers have been overcome by entrepreneurs who are already in the market.

In most cases private companies have not been able to operate in many states or within certain specific levels of corrections, such as high security prisons, because certain perceived barriers to entry exist, including the notion that private guards should not be placed in a position of having to make life and death decisions using deadly force against prison inmates, and a government's concern that once a contract is awarded to a private company the perceived difficulties in changing vendors places them at the mercy of the vendor who will in the long run raise per diem rates sharply, eliminating the possibility of savings resulting from competition. The opinions of private and public prison officials gathered during this study should prove useful in directing interested parties toward further research into the subject of prison market "entrance barriers".

Methodology

A cost-benefit analysis (CBA) is an analytical method for assessing the desirability of some prospective change. It involves the determination of all relevant costs and benefits, regardless of when they occur or to whom they accrue. A CBA would be inappropriate in studying privatization of prisons for two reasons: one, this study is not searching for "cheaper" methods to provide a particular service and two, it is not attempting to compare the benefits (output) of two different services. This study is attempting to determine whether similar programs (services, facilities) provided by the public and private sector cost the same or if one sector's costs are significantly lower.

A cost-effectiveness analysis (CEA) is also not appropriate for this study. A CEA is a procedure for identifying the least-cost means of achieving a given objective (Williams and Anderson 1975). In performing a CEA, one must be able to measure the effectiveness of the output of programs in some meaningful way and in a manner useful for comparing with the effectiveness of the output of programs or a single program over time. The well-worn prison effectiveness indicator, recidivism, has engendered considerable debate regarding its accuracy and reliability. This study is not concerned with determining how effective a program is or in measuring a program's per dollar ability to effectuate results. This study specifically attempts to measure costs and costs alone, for comparison purposes.

A cost-efficiency study (CES) is used in this research. The traditional approach used in an efficiency study is to divide total operating costs (dollars expended) by the number of clients (prisoners) (Hatry 1979). It is imperative that the prisons being compared be analyzed to determine their differences (levels of service and quantity of programs) so that cost comparisons can take on real meaning. Environmental factors impacting on the level of services rendered such as: differences in location, resource availability, local laws and policies, and extra or hidden costs, must be identified. One-time fixed and implicit costs must be identified and measured, using estimation techniques if real cost figures are not available. In recent years, efficiency studies have been used by governments to identify less efficient services and programs, to hold managers accountable over time for producing more efficiently, and for setting program standards, targets, and goals.

An efficiency study uses basic measurement units of dollars and/or employee hours per client. The study presented in chapter 4 is a comparison of the management of public and private prisons in terms of dollar expenditures. It maintains an awareness of operational activities, programs and services, inputs and environmental factors that might impact on any differences in costs that are determined. In addition, I have analyzed the direct and indirect costs making up total costs used in comparing the samples in the two sectors.

Summary of Chapters

Chapter 2 is a history of society's commitment to the privatization of public services. Included is a discussion of New York City's fiscal problems in the early 1970s, a forerunner of problems later experienced by many major industrial-commercial cities. Second, historical information is presented on the taxpayers' revolt, referred to by political, historical, and economic analysts as a period of growing emphasis by the public on decreasing tax expenditures and increasing governmental efficiency. Finally, a discussion on the antecedents to the current focus on "privatization" is presented, including the impact on OMB Circular A-76, and ending with a discussion on the meaning and determinants of privatization.

Chapter 3 presents a review of the current prison privatization movement. Included is a review of prison privatization from its origin to current trends. Major political, administrative, legal, financial, and social problems and impacts are identified and analyzed. Barriers to entry into the prison market as identified from research interviews are listed and evaluated.

Chapter 4 is a comparison of the costs of public and private prisons and a comparison of the views of public and private operators about barriers to entry into the private prison market. Chapter 4 places the results of these comparisons alongside the differences in service levels provided by the public and private prisons being compared.

Chapter 5 first discusses policy-making in general and how policy-making techniques apply to prison privatization. Included also are comments by public and private prison managers about problems and concerns typically offered by opponents of prison privatization.

Chapter 6 presents a summary and conclusions and clarifies whether an effort should be made by government toward increased contracting to private companies to manage prisons.

2

Privatization: History and Commitment in the United States

Historical Perspective

Every dollar that the government spends ought to be spent as carefully as if the resources of the country were limited. [A] vast deal remains to be done in the mere line of efficiency. Indeed, there has been very little serious effort even yet in the direction of making the government of the United States as efficient as a successful business organization would be.[1]

Woodrow Wilson's words are that of the twenty-eighteenth president but could easily be words spoken by George Bush, forty-first president. The Reagan and Bush administrations have repeated the privatization theme more often than any other administration. The privatization theme was a driving force behind the Reagan administration theory of government (Mclaughlin 1986). As a corollary to Reagan's supply-side economic policies, supply-side theorists such as Arthur Laffer, George Gilder, Judy Wanniski, and Jack Kemp have rediscovered Say's Law and classic economic postulates that recognize the importance and impact of incentives on the efficient production of services (particularly public services) (Poole 1982).

The Bush administration hopes to shrink the public sector relative to the private sector and revitalize the private sector's interest in producing services that are being produced by government. The administration expects to do this by extending privatization of public goods and services as a viable option to the public, as a means of providing superior services at less cost in taxpayer dollars (Butler 1984 and 1985). The Grace Commission's recommendations, to be detailed later, were a vehicle used by the Reagan administration to reach the objective of increased private sector involvement in the production and/or provision of government services. The Grace Commission's recommendations represent one of the strongest initiatives ever taken by an administration toward reaching the goals of privatization (Goodsell 1984).

New York City's Experience

The fiscal crisis in New York City in the mid-seventies is a significant contributor to the increased attention by governments upon the privatization of public goods and services. The New York City fiscal crisis magnified the linkage between fiscal fitness, government structure, type and quantity of services offered, and quality of life (Levine 1980). Studies about "retrenchment" and "cutback management" swelled overnight, many of them using the New York City crisis as a model.

New York City's experience can be viewed as occurring in four phases (Levine *et al* 1981). Until 1965, New York City experienced a stable political coalition, low interest-group participation, and moderate revenue growth. Between 1965 and 1970, however, New York City experienced rapid economic growth and increased public funds, such as increased categorical and formula grants, mostly resulting from revenues provided to cities through Johnson-era Great Society programs. During the period from 1970 to 1975, however, New York experienced a decline in revenues resulting from a decreased tax base and lower grant levels. The Nixon administration chose to provide block grants and general revenue sharing, at lower levels of funding, in place of many of the categorical formula and project grants that proliferated during the Johnson administration. The city then shifted to "cutting back" and employing fiscal restraint (Levine *et al* 1981). The city administration took steps to revamp inefficient services, cut back services across the board, refinance debt, and reduce the total number of government employees.

The period since 1975 in New York City has been a period of service rationing, reduced intergovernmental aid, the pursuit of efficiency and productivity, and the transferring of responsibility for the production of social services to the private sector or to other governments, which for cities included increased user fees, program elimination, and the transfer of many social programs to the state. New York City was not alone in its attempt to decrease fiscal stress. Cities across the nation were and are experiencing fiscal stress due to declining tax bases and lower levels of federal aid. Nevertheless, many cities have been developing ways to cope with the ever-present conflict between the pressure to satisfy greater social needs with decreased funds.

Taxpayers' Revolt

Like the cities, many states felt the pressure for tax relief. In 1978, Proposition 13 was developed by California Realtor Howard Jarvis, who led a grass roots citizens' drive for tax relief. California's taxpayers argued that elected officials should stop the growing tax burden and decrease property taxes, the base from which most municipal services and programs are funded.

For many years California's taxes had been increasing at rates far higher than the percentage increase in growth of national production, measured by GNP (see Table 2.1).[2] The 1977 California tax assessment, for example, had increased 14.5 per cent, higher than any increase in assessment in twenty years ("Tax Payer Revolt: Where..." 1978). President Carter cited the California spending growth and tax increases in his 1978 budget address and threatened to aim new vetoes at congressional increases of budgeted programs. President Carter stated that 40 per cent of national income was going to one in five workers in the labor force, specifically government workers, and government spending was too high.

Table 2.1
Average Annual Rate of Increases in State and Local
Taxes Compared to Increases in GNP

ITEM	1953–58	1958–63	1963–68	1968–73	1973–78
Total state and local taxes	7.8%	7.7%	9.0%	12.4%	10.1%
State income tax	9.8	13.9	16.3	20.1	13.8
State sales tax	7.8	9.6	13.5	13.6	11.8
Local property tax	8.4	7.2	7.0	10.4	8.2
GNP Increases	4.2	5.5	7.5	8.3	9.9

Source: Will Myers, "Proposition 13: Nationwide Implication," *National Tax Journal* 32 (1979): p. 172.

Californians also believed that state government spending was too high. Proposition 13 was passed in California in June of 1978 by 65 per cent of the voters (Summers 1979, 5). Proposition 13 included several important measures to control spending: (1) property taxes could not be increased more than one percent of the average market value of homes; (2) only by a 2/3 vote by the California legislature could public service expenditures be increased; and (3) local property taxes were to be reduced by more than one-half (Ladd 1978). Supporters of the Jarvis initiative were columnist William Buckley and economists Dr. S. Milton Friedman and Neil Jacoby. These men made the argument that "waste from government results because of attempts to produce private goods and public goods by regulation of the private sector" which "inefficiently forces the production of undesired goods." "Waste in government deals with inefficiency in spending and raising revenues" (Hagman 1978, 39–40).

Richard Musgrave observed that other reasons existed for the development of Proposition 13: (1) California's unusually brisk housing boom; (2) the unusually efficient state assessment procedures resulting in the rapid rise in assessed values; (3) a large state accumulated budget surplus; and (4) the state's lag time for providing property tax relief (Musgrave 1979). The State was too slow to use surplus funds. Californians' real income was declining while the tax burden was increasing. In addition, several other factors triggered California's tax revolt: (1) the economy was experiencing inflation and increasing interest rates; (2) the public climate remained in favor of income redistribution goals (which placed a large burden on government provision of services); (3) lobby groups were forcing a number of increased expenditures issues; (4) government analysts underestimated program costs; and (5) the general incentive for government bureaucracies was and has always been program growth. Taxpayers in California and other states wanted to reduce government inefficiency, reform state and local tax laws, and restrain the size of government (Summers 1979).

California's initiatives were a harbinger of more states' tax limitation laws to follow. In 1979, according to the polls, Michigan voters believed government was too large (Courant 1980, 2). Public employee wages and benefits were on the average higher than competitive salaries in the private sector. Government was seen as inefficient, operating inside the production possibilities curve (Courant 1980). The Michigan tax revolt was also seen as an initiative against welfare spending, which ironically is a type of spending that in Michigan (as it is in most other states) is financed about equally by federal, state, and local governments. Michigan's 1979 "Proposal E", stated:

(1) State revenues would be limited to their current proportion of personal income.
(2) Local governments would be protected against sudden state decreases in funding.

(3) Increases in local taxes would require voter approval.
(4) No increase in property taxes would occur without voter approval..

Also, Proposal E would immediately decrease property taxes and limit future property tax increases to 2½ percent growth per year (Niskanen 1979).

Another example of state tax revolt initiatives was Proposition 2½, enacted by the Commonwealth of Massachusetts in 1980 (Moscovitch 1985). The objectives of Proposition 2½ were to:

(1) force local governments to look at spending priorities and take advantage of state revenues;
(2) limit property taxes to 2½% of "full and fair" market values and;
(3) increase local government innovation and efficiency (hopefully through privatization) vis-a-vis decreased State funds.

If local fee revenues or state aid did not increase, a 2½ per cent cap on tax increases in the face of five per cent inflation meant a net decrease in public services barring more efficient spending (Moscovitch 1985).

The impact of Proposition 2½ on local governments in Massachusetts was significant. Locals increased their use of the bidding process by bidding for services such as insurance, where once the contract was a non-bid contract, resulting in a sharp decrease in insurance rates. School officials are now required to produce two budgets: one budget reflects a "bare bones" estimate, the second budget reflects a "bare bones plus five percent increase" estimate. Local governments have increased user fees and statute fees wherever possible for permits, inspections, and entrance fees, to offset the need for increased taxes while continuing to provide certain services. "There can be little doubt that Proposition 2½ spending limits forced (or helped) [Massachusetts] to make some overdue changes", says Edward Moscovitch (1985).

In the period of 1978–80, following the enactment of Proposition 13 in California, taxpayers saved over $30 billion in decreased taxes. There was an explosive growth in private sector jobs. More than 930,000 jobs were created in the private sector during these two years ("Proposition..." 1982). By 1982, more than twenty states had enacted spending caps, over half of which began as grass roots efforts (Stanfield 1983, 2568-72). The combined effects of recession and inflation, coupled with lower federal support, contributed to the taxpayers' revolt. Inflation, it appears, bends the political climate to the right, climaxing in anti-public sector sentiments and attitudes. On the expenditure side, individuals become dissatisfied with benefits they receive as real incomes decrease. Moreover, taxpayers become unhappy about paying for an increased measure of benefits that others receive (Muscgrave 1979).

A 1978 Gallup opinion poll measured taxpayers' opinions regarding several relevant issues. Everette Ladd sums up the results of the Gallup Poll by saying:

> [Taxpayers] want lower taxes. They want government to perform better than it has. They want it to spend more prudently. And they want it to maintain a high level of public services. (Ladd 1978, 29)

Figure 2.1 presents several of the Gallup Poll questions and their responses (Ladd 1978, 29–33).

George Break interpreted the taxpayers' revolt by noting:

> To a close observer of the Proposition 13 movement, both before and after the election, it is simply not clear whether it attracted votes mainly as a means of attacking "big Government" and taxes in general, as Howard Jarvis and others quickly claimed in the aftermath of the vote, or simply as a way of protesting the recent heavy overload of the property tax. . . . The differences between these two possible interpretations of what the public wants are critically important, as decisions following from the prevailing one will have far reaching consequences for the state. (Break 1979, 43)

Figure 2.1
Gallup Poll: Questions and Responses Regarding Taxes

Question: "From your personal standpoint, please tell me for each tax that I read off to you if you feel it is too high, too low, or about right."

Response:	Too High				
	1969	1973	1975	1977	1978
Federal Income Tax	66%	64%	72%	69%	70%
State Income Tax	40	53	53	41	55
Local Property Tax	62	68	55	66	64
State Sales Tax	60	56	53	51	45

Question:	Which Taxes have increased a great deal?	
Response:	Real Estate Tax	58%
	Sales Tax	25%
	Income Tax	36%
Question:	Which is the fairest tax?	
Response:	Real Estate Tax	10%

Sales Tax   43%
Income Tax   36%

Question: Do you think people in government waste a lot of money we pay in taxes?

Response: "Yes, [they] waste a lot"

1958	46%	1972	67%
1964	48%	1974	76%
1968	61%	1976	76%
1970	70%	1978	80%

Question: Two weeks ago, voters in California passed Proposition 13, which reduced property taxes by more than half....Would you vote for it?

Response:

	For	Against	Wouldn't Vote	No Opinion
	51%	24%	12%	13%
(By political ideology)				
Liberal	57	22	12	9
Moderate	52	27	11	9
Conservative	54	23	11	10

Question: Which government do you feel wastes the biggest part of the budget?

Response:

Federal	67%
State	14%
Local	5%
No Response	14%

Source: 1978 Gallup Opinion Poll in Everette Ladd, "The Tax Revolt," *Public Opinion* (July/August 1978): 29–34.

Cutback Management

Phenomena such as urban fiscal stress, decreasing federal funding, service shedding, and the taxpayers' revolt have promoted a growing movement in all levels of government to retrench or regroup in terms of how to spend limited amounts of revenue on a growing agenda of services and programs (Nathan 1985). The following statement by Finance Committee Chairman Russell Long (D—La.), exemplified the mood in Congress in 1980:

The Senate Finance Committee began its own hearings a day later under orders from nervous Senate Democrats to come up with a tax bill by September 3. It is safe to say this side of the aisle—certainly in this Committee and I think in the Senate as a whole—favors a tax cut voted this year. ("Tax Cut..." 1980, 40–41)

Small federal income tax decreases, however, have little overall impact on the total proportion of income allocated to taxes. Income revenues are approximately 3/10 of the revenue received from all taxes. As table 2.2 illustrates, voters are currently taxed through at least seventy tax mechanisms, most of which are not "income taxes," and the total revenue of which is close to $1 trillion dollars ("Still No Rest..." 1984, 60).

Table 2.2
Tax Mechanisms

Federal Taxes

Individual Income	Miscellaneous Excise
Corporate Income	Telephone, teletype
Social Insurance	Foreign Insurance
Social Security	Foundations
Railroad Retirement	Wagering
State Unemployment	Employees pension
Federal Unemployment	Other Excise
Railroad Unemployment	Airports and rails
Federal Retirement	Highway Trust Funds
	Gasoline
	Trucks, buses, trailer
	Tires, rubber
Alcohol	Diesel fuels
Distilled Spirits	Vehicles Use Tax
Beer	Truck parts
Wine	Oils
Special taxes	Other Trust Funds
	Black lung
Tobacco	Inland waterways
Cigarettes	Hazardous substances
Cigars	Estates and Gifts
Other products	Customs and duties
Manufactures Excise	
Windfall profits (oil)	
Gasoline	
Firearms and ammunition	
Fishing products	
Gas Guzzler tax	

Local Taxes	State Taxes
Individual	Sales and Gross Receipts
Corporate	General
General sales	Motor fuels
Motor fuels	Corporations
Alcoholic beverages	Hunting, fishing
Tobacco	Drivers
Public utilities	Alcoholic beverages
Other taxes	Other
Property taxes	Individual Income
	Corporate Income
	Severance
	Property
	Estate, Gift
	Other Taxes

Source: Compiled from tables in "Still No Rest For The Poor", *U.S. News and World Report* 60 (7 May 1984): 60.

As stated earlier, the Reagan administration brought to the White House a set of goals that included a reduction of regulations, increased privatization of public services, increased vigilance toward fraud, waste and abuse, and a reduction of taxes. In 1985, the Gallup organization completed a poll to determine voter agreement with Reagan's (conservative) tax proposal ("Reagan's Tax..." 1985, 14–30). The results were:

	Favor	Oppose	No Opinion
Nationally	49%	29%	22%

The poll may have reflected the fact that the tax revolt was not only an indication of resentment of high property taxes but a mandate for a wide range of tax and expenditure changes. The public favored the Reagan policies that opposed increased social welfare (upholding the worke ethic), decreased aid to cities (where much of the "welfare" problems are concentrated), increased defense spending (reflective of conservative but aggressive national policy), decreased federal grants, and provided for deregulation and privatization (Nathan 1985). Reagan's 1986 budget proposal decreased grants to state and local governments by $9.7 billion, more than 9 per cent. Cuts included reduced monies for housing assistance, mass transit, sewer grants, energy conservation, and the elimination of Urban Development Action Grants used for revitalization of urban areas. Reagan's policies also included ending several agencies such as the Small Business Administration, the Economic Development Administration, Amtrak, the

Weatherization Program, and new public housing (Blakely 1986). He was successful in ending only the latter two programs.

According to Public Choice theorist Charles H. Levine (1986, 197):

> The deadlock between demands for government funds and services and insufficient resources needed to pay for them seems irresolvable from the vantage point of the mid-1980s.

The Bush and Reagan administration policies reflect an attempt to reverse the trends of the 1970s, which included a faltering economy, lower production, increased inflation, high interest rates, high unemployment, and increased taxes (Rubin 1985). President Reagan indicated that his administration intended to decrease government except for defense related programs. He stated:

> My Administration [sought] to limit the size, intrusiveness and cost of federal activities as much as possible and to achieve the needed increase in defense capabilities in the most cost-efficient manner possible. (Rubin 1985, 1)

The Bush administration's proposals and alternatives included more than just supply-side, tax-decrease programs of Reagan's era, such as the ERTA (Economic Recovery Tax Act of 1981), which included annual tax decreases. The Reagan administration's proposals included other retrenchment schemes such as a reduction of federal personnel, the deregulation of regulated industries (strict guidelines have been developed for agencies which develop regulations from legislation), weakened enforcement powers of some regulatory agencies, further consolidation of categorical grants into block grants, a decrease in total grant dollars, privatization of some public services as recommended by Reagan's Presidential Private Sector Survey on Cost Control (PPSSCC—popularly known as the Grace Commission), and the appointment of loyal program directors who can implement conservative spending policies (Rubin 1985, 199). The Bush administration continues to follow these same focuses.

At the local level, "cutback management" became a household word. Federal policy changes, initiatives, loss of federal funding, and a lingering recession required local managers tor redesign methods of management that had been originally designed during times of growth. This meant utilizing innovative policies that were applicable to circumstances of unlimited wants and scarce resources. According to Charles H. Levine (1980), the six most common cutback methods used at the local level are: fixing seniority as the criterion to determine who remains employed, implementing hiring freezes, making equal percentage cuts across programs, evaluating productivity criteria, cutting low productive units or people, and imposing zero-based budgeting techniques which allows both politics and analysis to become part of the decision-making process.

Anthony Downs formulated the following list of cutback methods, which he calls "coping strategies," that can be employed when governments are facing revenue reductions without concomitant reductions in demand (Downs 1981). Governments, he said, can raise taxes, reduce the level of services, produce services with lower costs, tighten the link between those who benefit and those who pay, and change the nature of the service demanded so as to produce less of it, such as converting welfare to workfare.

According to David T. Stanley (1980), the methods that cities may use to deal with long-term revenue decline include: using better and more appropriate fiscal methods and processes, exploring better revitalization tactics including other funding sources, load sharing, service shedding, cutting expenditures, using privatization methods including contracting out, voucher, systems, volunteerism, user fees, and identifying alternative revenue resources such as property and service taxes, licenses and permits, fines, forfeitures and penalties, service charges, utilities and enterprises, and assessments and loans. State and local governments have been able to identify other non-local revenue and non-revenue sources such as state aid, county and city financial relationship rearrangements, foundation funding, the use of joint agencies, service contracts, cooperative authorities, easements, law modifications, financial cooperations, and compulsory joint cooperation to assist them in coping with the loss of federal monies and reduced local revenues.

In trying to save money, local governments have found trash collection to be an example of a service for which they have been finding innovative methods of production (Savas 1980, 293). There are a number of methods for local governments to provide trash collection services other than municipal collection. These include contracting out, granting a franchise, providing private pickup, and permitting self-service. Emanuel S. Savas has found that contracting out for trash collection is the most cost-effective strategy for local governments. He writes:

Contract collection is least costly, franchise is next with municipal and private collection last. Municipal costs 15 percent more than contract. [This] discredits the belief that government can do it cheaper because there is no profit. (Savas 1980, 297)

Governments will need new solutions to problems of how to manage themselves more effectively. Charles Levine (1980) indicates that the alternatives to the conflict between scarce resources and growing wants for public services in the United States may depend on reducing defense spending through stronger military agreements with Russia (which are obviously unnecessary now), utilizing economic policies to reduce the federal deficit, electing officials to office who will reduce overall spending, and reducing the cost of government through privatization. Privatization is especially appealing in that it is a concrete method that can be used for redirecting production to the private sector while at the same time maintaining services, bypassing slow bureaucratic lag problems, and securing scarce technological talant that is usually located in the private sector.

Cutback management has its negative side. Reduction in one area always impacts on other functions or agencies. Data collection and analytic capabilities tend to get cut first—tools that are especially useful in the management process. Talented people tend to leave government during hard times, making this important resource scarce. Managing programs becomes difficult if not impossible when programs have a high probability of being terminated or amputated. Austerity generally translates into no productivity improvements. A conflict arises between mandated services and the lack of money to perform them. Also it is difficult to cut efficient programs that show promise. There are few rewards for conserving resources in public management.

The consensus among many theorists is for local public managers to develop innovative skills for developing alternatives to their current mix of revenue resources and program provision. A major alternative, it is argued, should be privatization.

OMB Circular A-76

The general policy of the United States government is to rely on commercial sources to supply the products and services the federal government needs. This policy was reaffirmed by the White House statement:

> The role of government should not include performing services and activities that can effectively be carried out by the private sector, and we will work for policies which increase reliance on the private sector.[3]

The guidelines utilized by recent national administrations for ensuring effective use of the private sector to produce the goods and services it needs are set forth in OMB Circulator No. A-76,

"Performance of Commercial Activities", developed and promulgated in 1955. This circular requires that competition be injected into the government procurement system and that efficiency be sought through private sector production.

The circular establishes a method of measurement for determining which services should be produced by the private sector and which services should be produced by the public sector. The circular does not mandate contracting out, but challenges public managers to be cost-efficient and maximally productive (Poole 1984). The circular rests on three precepts: retention of governmental functions in-house, achievement of economies and productivity through competition, and reliance on the commercial sector.

The last precept is the most relevant. The circular requires periodic evaluation of all federally-produced commercial activities to determine their efficiency. Traditionally, commercial activities produced by the federal government are extensive and include activities such as painting and paperhanging, operating industrial equipment, preparing and serving foods, plumbing and pipefitting, metalwork, warehousing goods, laundry work, performing computer maintenance, engineering and architecture work, maintaining libraries and archives, and doing electrical work. Many of these activities can be privatized.

OMB Circular A-76 asks the question: Which activities are commercial and which are government functions? It helps administrators determine which functions should remain in-house, to perform regularly scheduled cost studies between private and public sectors, and solicit locally-approved business where possible—reviewing activities that have expanded more than thirty percent (Office of Management and Budget 1985).

The administration's emphasis on OMB Circular A-76 has contributed to the Office of Management and Budget's ability to play a controlling role in the administration's monitoring of services. In addition, OMB Circular A-95 (now rescinded and replaced with Executive Order 12372 in fiscal year 1982) requires OMB to monitor state clearinghouses that were designed to centralize requests for funds, to ensure against overlap. Currently, changes to regulations and other management proposals, such as those proposed by the Grace Commission, are to be funnelled through OMB, a Bush administration safeguard against proliferating regulations and rules (Gordon 1986).

Privatization

A number of alternatives have been identified that should resolve or at least diffuse conflict between the increasing public mandate for social programs and the decreasing amount of funds available to produce them. The advent of a revised version of OMB A-76 promulgated in 1983, the Grace Commission findings, and increased local use of alternative provision schemes such as contracting-out and vouchers have combined to focus a great deal of attention on the privatization of public services.

The term "privatization" conjures up images of transferring public services to the private sector and having the private sector responsible for the provision and production of public services. Misconceptions about privatization abound. A recent Gallup poll shows how well the public understands the implications of privatization (see table 2.3).

Table 2.3
Popular Perceptions of the Effect of Privatization

Privatization:	yes	no	no change	don't know
	%	%	%	%
Increases profits for owners	84	4	4	8
Makes firms more likely to develop new products	59	11	17	13
Gives more attention to customers	46	15	30	9
Makes firms better run	43	13	32	11
Worsens conditions for workers	30	17	38	15
Lowers prices	22	14	54	11

Source: Gallup Poll, *Political Index* no. 337 (September 1988), p. 20.

Privatization means different things to different people, the determinants of which depend upon such factors as the country one is in, the sector (private or public) where one's interests lie, attitudes toward government (liberal or conservative), and the economic philosophy one agrees with (Keynesian, Friedmanian, Smithian, et cetera). I will here provide a definition of privatization and a list of conditions and circumstances that might call for privatization. Later, a general definition linking the common traits of the most relevant traditional definitions will be established and utilized to decribe the Grace Commission's recommendations, as well as further used in following chapters to analyze the prison privatization movement.

The literature of privatization tends to explain privatization on one of two levels. The first level of explanation is essentially ideological—one is for privatization because he is in favor of a laissez-faire state. The second level of explanation of privatization is essentially analytical—one supports privatization as a way of controlling government expenditures. Developing a definition of privatization depends somewhat upon which level of explanation one agrees with (Tuckman 1985).

In the ideological approach, discussion of privatization revolves around arguments regarding freedom of choice, freedom from government control, and the failures of the welfare state. According to Vincent and Elinor Ostrom's discourse on Public Choice theory (1977), the larger government becomes relative to the commercial sector, the more the public's choices are translated into government controls. Although the process is subtle and incremental, it continues, nevertheless, if not challenged. James Bennett and Manuel Johnson (1980) contend that as government grows in terms of income collected as taxes as a proportion of GNP, there occurs a loss of consumer sovereignty and a decline in the guiding function of prices. According to authorities on the "welfare state," it is not a sine qua non that government must be the offerer of welfare programs.[4] If anything, government production and provision results in failures of several kinds. Mini Abramovitz (1986, 257) states that the welfare state is "built on the principle of service provision, outside the market, on the basis of need. . . ."

Abramovitz argues that government failures include government inefficiently taking profits from the private sector, bureaucrats building empires, state ownership (world-wide) leading to mismanagement (which leads to reduced program quality), capital flight, and migration. Abramovitz cites as government failures the existence of bureaucratic and political constraints to the delivery of services and extra costs for the provision of services that are not generally counted as costs such as legislative oversight and auditing (Abramovitz, 1986; Bennett and Johnson 1980; Schlesinger et al. 1986; Leat 1986; Hanke 1985).

The second level of explanation of privatization the analytical approach, emanates from an evaluation of program provision and production in terms of classical economic theory, especially efficiency theory. It is upon this type of analytical reasoning that the arguments for privatization of prisons, established in later chapters, are based. There are incentives inherent in private enterprise, typically absent from government enterprise, which lower the costs of privately-produced goods and services that are collectively consumed. The self-interest motives being absent, attempts are being made to install them within the public provision of services (Cook and Elkin 1985). There is evidence that because of the economic incentives that self-interest provides, the private sector can deliver better services at a lower cost. The private sector decision-maker has the greatest incentive to take all benefits and costs into account (Chi 1985; Hanke 1985). "The degree of competition that a [market] arrangement permits will, to a significant degree, determine how efficiently that arrangement will supply a service" (Savas 1982). Howard P. Tuckman concludes that there are five component parts to privatization based upon analytical reasoning of economic theory. The five component parts include: a reduction in the size of the public sector, an introduction of greater competition into the provision of collective services, a greater use of incentives to foster private for public production, and streamlining outputs from collectively provided services (Tuckman 1985).

With the main elements as stated above in mind, privatization may be defined as the increasing of private sector involvement, relative to public sector involvement, in programs available to the public. One must be careful in using the terms "providing" or "producing" when discussing privatization. Ted Kolderie explains that it is a policy decision to "provide" services and an administrative decision to "produce" services. Either provision or production or both can be the responsibility of either the public or private sector. A government's approach to service depends upon the responsibilities they are willing, able, or required to accept or delegate. Table 2.4 shows several approaches to service availability by different mixes of responsibility for provision and production of services (Kolderie 1986).

In the United States, governmental commitment to privatization is not one of "service shedding," that is, alleviating itself of the responsibility for both provision and production. In most cases, at the federal, state, and local levels, the privatization movement is toward decreasing responsibility for provision of services or eliminating responsibility for production, but not both. This is the same view taken by governments opting to privatize prisons. They wish to take advantage of the benefits of private sector production but would continue to provide the prison service to the community.

Table 2.4
Provision/Production By Sector

Approach	Responsibility	
	Provision	Production
All Private Sector	P	P
Contracting	G	P
User Fees	P	G
All Public Sector	G	G
P = Private Sector		
G = Public Sector		

Source: Compiled from data presented in Ted Kolderie, "The Two Different Concepts of Privatization," *Public Administration Review* (July/August); 1986.

Emanuel S. Savas, Harry Hatry, Robert Poole, and Madsen Pirie have developed different typologies of arrangements for the delivery of local government services. Savas's typology of delivery arrangements is based upon two dimensions: "consumption" and "exclusion" (Savas 1982, 34). Collective goods (national defense, television) are jointly consumed and exclusion is not possible. Toll goods (cable television) have a joint consumption characteristic but exclusion from use is possible. Private goods (television sets, automobiles) are privately consumed and exclusion is possible. Common pool goods (clean air, benefits from polio vaccine) are privately consumed and exclusion is not possible. Savas examines a number of institutionalized arrangements for service delivery by types of goods (private, toll, collective, common pool) that align themselves best (see table 2.5) and concludes that many goods and services now produced by the public sector and treated as collective goods are really toll or common pool goods that would more efficiently be produced by contracting with the private sector.

Table 2.5
Service Delivery By Types Of Goods

Arrangement	Private Goods	Toll Goods	Common P. Goods	Collective Goods
Government Svs.		X	X	X
Government Agreement		X	X	X
Contract for Svs.		X	X	X
Franchise		X		
Grants	X	X	X	
Vouchers	X	X	X	
Self Service	X			
Market	X	X		

Source: Compiled from data in Emanuel S. Savas, *Privatizing The Public Sector* (Chatham, N.J.: Chatham House Publishers, 1982). Savas' 1987 book, *Privatization: The Key To Better Government*, expands on this table. This version is more useful here as it explains more simply how various goods can have a variety of delivery mechanisms.

Savas expands on his description of service delivery arrangements by separating them into categories of goods and services separated by sector of responsibility (see figure 2.2).

Figure 2.2
Overview of ten Institutional
Arrangements For Delivering Services

Goods and Services

Government Arranges		Private Sector Arranges	
Govt Produces	Private Produces	Private Produces	Govt Produces
1 govt Svs	1 contract	1 voucher	1 govt
2 inter-	2 franchise	2 market	vendor
govt	3 grant	3 volunteer	
agreement		4 self svs.	

Source: Donahue, John D. *The Privatization Decision* (New York: Basic Books, 1989), 139–40.

Harry Hatry's typology of arrangements for the delivery of services is worth mentioning. He has related each delivery approach to one or more given impacts that may occur (see table 2.6).[5] Harry Hatry argues that local officials must become service "brokers" rather than service "producers," concerned with the provision of services regardless of how they are delivered.

Table 2.6
Approaches To Service Delivery and Their Possible Impacts

Approaches

1. Contract for services (a)
2. Franchise (licensing) (b)
3. Grants and Subsidies (c)
4. Vouchers (c, e)
5. Volunteers (b)
6. Self help (c)
7. Regulation (tax changes) (a)
8. Private sector takeover (service shedding) (c)
9. Reduce demand (a)
10. Private enterprise help (executive aid) (b)
11. User fees and charges (a, d)

Impacts

a. Services at lower cost
b. Reduce demand on the government

c.   Reduce service (without reducing demand)
d.   Increase revenues
c.   Increase amount, quality, effectiveness of services

Source: Compiled from data located in Harry P. Hatry, *Private Approaches For Delivery Of Public Services* (Washington, D.C.: Urban Institute, 1983), chapter 1.

The Grace Commission

It is important to include here a somewhat more detailed discussion of the Grace Commission prior to any discussion on privatization of prisons, as many of the arguments used to persuade Congress to initiate privatization legislation generally have been used to support the privatization of prisons argument. When the Federal Government takes the lead by implementing federal initiatives, states tend to follow the lead, which helps states in prioritizing their goals. The Reagan administration's priorities were consistent with the Bush administration's first-term priorities, which include: eliminating fraud, waste, and abuse, reducing agency administration of program costs, reducing federal employment, combining and condensing periodicals and publications (there were sixteen thousand publications in 1981; four thousand have now been eliminated), decreasing unnecessary printing, reducing of government personnel travel, reducing office space, consolidating the pay systems, improving financial management, increasing OMB A-76 reviews and making program delivery improvements (Office of Management and Budget 1987). Most of these priorities are reflected in the goals of the Grace Commission.

President Reagan's Executive Order of 30 June 1982, to establish the Grace commission recruited 161 executives from the private sector. The conceptual framework for the President's Private Sector Survey on Cost Control (PPSSCC—a.k.a. the Grace Commission) is based upon the idea that government should provide certain services, but if possible, not produce them. If the government chooses to provide a service using the private sector, there are options to choose from including contracting, providing a grant or subsidy, using tax incentives as an inducement, decreasing regulations such that company production costs are lower, providing vouchers so as to perpetuate competition, and granting a franchise.

Contracting was found by the Grace Commission to be the most common and fruitful method of privatization of the delivery of federal goods and services. A survey conducted by the International City Manager's Association (U.S. Congress, Subcommittee on Monetary and Fiscal Policy 1984) found that of 1780 cities surveyed, 41 per cent used contracting to provide for removal of commercial waste, 34 per cent used contracting for removal of residential solid waste, 30 per cent for tree trimming, 78 per cent for vehicle towing and storage, and 20 per cent for fleet management. Many municipalities are also contracting out for the management of hospitals. The Commission concluded that contracting for services could produce a savings of tax dollars of as much as $424.4 billion, if all of their findings were implemented. The Commission found that when the government and private sector produced similar services, the government's costs were higher. They found a lacking of incentives on the part of public agencies to operate efficiently was the cause of this. Inefficiently managed agencies tend to receive funds and staff at the same levels as efficiently managed agencies. Additionally, powerful constituencies exist within and outside of the government that can and do effectively lobby to prevent change of the status quo. A corollary to the above findings is that vested interests and political pressures exert more force in the managerial decision-making process than can be effectively measured. Government administrations feel more strongly the impact of political redress than administrative inefficiency (U.S. Congress, Subcommittee on Monetary and Fiscal Policy 1984).

The Grace Commission included some political strategies among their formal recommendations regarding privatization (President's Private Sector Survey on Cost Control 1983). These were: (1) The President should establish a high level privatization group in the Office of Federal Management (OFM). The group would be responsible for the continuing privatization process by making evaluations of the resent process and recommending new privatization measures. (2) The President should establish a key administrative management office in each department or agency with responsibility for identification, review, analysis and implementation of privatization opportunities. (3) The Office of Federal Management should develop procedures that would facilitate private sector initiatives to identify which services are candidates for privatization.

Contracting For Services

Information collected in this study indicates that the privatization method determined as most efficient by the PPSSCC and most relevant to prisons is contracting. Prisons at all levels currently contract for many services within their structure, and there are already a number of fully privately-contracted correction facilities (mostly juvenile facilities and maximum security jails). Savas (1987) writes that "contracting costs less and provides the same or a better quality of service," according to table 2.7 developed in a survey completed by Floristano and Gordin (1980).

Table 2.7
Survey of Public Officials' Opinions About contracting

Opinion service	Small Jurisdiction	Large Jurisdiction
Costs less	40%	41%
Costs same	19%	22%
Costs more	34%	10%
Better service	63%	33%
Same service	14%	48%
Poorer service	22%	15%

Small jurisdictions = population < 50,000, N = 89.
Large jurisdictions = population < 500,000 N = 14.

Sources: Patricia S. Florestano and Stephen B. Gordon, "Public vs. Private: Small government contracting with the Private Sector," *Public Administration Review* 40 (January/February 1980): 29–43; Patricia S. Florestano and Stephen B. Gordon, "Private Provision of Public Services: Contracting by Large Local governments," International Journal of Public Administration, no. 3 (1979): 307–27; also Savas 1987, 112.

According to Harry P. Hatry, governments that contract for services (as opposed to keeping services in-house) benefit in number of ways (Hatry 1983). They experience lower personnel costs due to lower pensions and benefits. They are able to avoid the bureaucratic red tape associated with the delivery of service. They can avoid construction delays. They can explore new technologies that are sometimes open to private industries and not yet available to the public sector. They meet their needs quickly for short-term expert assistance. Contracting out, then, allows a government to continue to provide a service by financing, regulating, evaluating, and controlling it without producing or delivering the service (Pirie 1985).

Emanuel Savas points out some of the arguments made against contracting. First is that contracting out allows less direct control over services by a public provider. Second, contracting may be objectionable on the grounds that contracts are very susceptible to labor disputes and corporate financial failures. Thirdly, private production is said to be more costly due to the added cost of normal profits (Savas 1982).

Regardless of the arguments for and against privatization, there have evolved a number of cost studies that report contracting out as having produced substantial savings over municipal or state delivery of services as seen in table 2.8 (Moore 1987, 63). These studies have been performed by both government and private agencies. In addition, Steven Moore reports that several cities cite contracting out as the reason for multi-million-dollar savings in tax expenditures or government expenses (Moore 1987, 63).

— Phoenix saved $5.3 million annually in contracting for services;
— Southern California municipalities saved $4.5 million by contracting out bus transportation;
— Los Angeles, since Proposition 13, has issued over two hundred contracts and saved $200,000 million; and
— Elk Grove, Illinois saved $200,000 from contracting out for fire fighting.

Table 2.8
Cost Estimates From Contracting For Services:
Studies Conducted Since 1981

Author of Study	Type of Study	% Savings
HUD (Ecodata)	Municipal street cleaning	43%
HUD (Ecodata)	Municipal janitorial services	73%
HUD (Ecodata)	Municipal tree trimming	37%
HUD (Ecodata)	Municipal construction	96%
HUD (Ecodata)	Municipal traffic light maintenance	56%
American Public Works Association	Wide range of services	39%
U.S. Department of Transportation	Urban mass transit	35–50%
E. S. Savas	Refuse collection	30%
Steve Hanke	Waste water treatment	20–50%
Martin Sellers	Private prison management	62%

Sources: Steven Moore, "Contracting Out," in Steve H. Hanke (ed.), *Prospects For Privatization* (New York: Academy of Political Science, 1987), p. 63.

John Donahue (1989) presents us with the results of a 1984 study performed by Barbara Stevens and the Department of Housing and Urban Development. That study is "the source of the much repeated finding that municipal agencies are 50 percent less efficient than private contractors." Tables developed from that study show how much more services cost when performed by a municipal government rather than a private firm (see tables 2.9 and 2.10).

Table 2.9
Estimated Gains from Privatization

Function	Extra Cost of Municipal Service Over the Cost of Contractor Service
	(percent)
Asphalt overlay construction	96
Janitorial services	73
Traffic signal maintainance	56
Street cleaning	43
Trash collection	42
Turf maintenance	40
Tree maintenance	37
Payroll preparaton	0

Source: Barbara J. Stevens, "Comparing Public and Private Sector privatization Efficiency: An Analysis of Eight Activities," *National Productivity Review* (Autumn 1984): 401, table 5.

Table 2.10
How Agencies and Contractors Differ In Costs

	Cities Using Contractors	Cities Using Agencies
Direct labor share of costs	49.0%	60.2%
Workforce unionized	20.0%	48.1%
Average age of workers	32.1	36.1
Average job tenure (yrs)	5.8	8.1
Vacation days per worker	10.1	14.0
Average absenteeism (days)	8.8	12.9
Management layers	1.5	1.9
Foremen can fire workers	53.7%	16.0%
Written reprimands used	33.8%	72.5%
Employee incentive system	26.9%	12.3%
Workers maintain own equipment	92.5%	48.1%
Formal staff meetings held	53.8%	81.5%

Source: Barbara J. Stevens, "Delivering Municipal Services Efficiently" (Washington, D.C.: Department of Housing and Urban Development, Office of Policy Development and Research, 1984), 18–19.

In summary, the lessons learned from New York City's fiscal crisis, the Taxpayers' Revolt, and retrenchment and cutback management, as well as the Federal Government's use of regulatory tools such as

Circular A-76 and survey efforts like PPSSCC, have caused government leaders to focus a critical eye upon whether programs can be produced more cheaply by the private sector.

However, getting public officials to move in a real way toward implementing privatization alternatives is another story. Jeffrey Henig writes,

> Establishing the feasibility of a genuinely new proposal can present a *Catch-22* situation. Until the idea is put into practice, assessments of feasibility necessarily are speculative and hypothetical. But elected officials usually resist adopting new ideas backed only by speculation and hypothesis. (Henig 1990, 656)

With this groundwork having been laid, the next chapter explores events leading up to the current attention given to the privatization of prisons. The first part of chapter 3 is a discussion of the history of the privatization of prisons movement and the influence that contracting has had upon the corrections industry. The remainder of chapter 3 will include a discussion on the current status of contracting for entire prison management systems.

3

The Prison Privatization Movement

Why has the idea of privatization of prisons drawn so much attention in the 1980s? Conceptually and empirically there are several reasons for society's increased attention upon, and movement toward, greater private industry responsibility for corrections. Historically, law enforcement and the administration of justice through corrections rested entirely on the shoulders of the state. Persons accused of crimes are made to await trial. In the court system, convicted criminals are remanded to jails or prisons to serve sentences and to be rehabilitated. The criminal justice system has, in the late 1970s to the present day, moved toward broadening and diversifying the meaning, scope, and methods for carrying out penal sanctions imposed by society on criminals (National Institute of Law Enforcement and Criminal Justice 1978, 1).

Conceptually, the criminal justice system has been in need, over the last fifteen years, of expanding and increasing the use of halfway houses, parole, probation, work-release programs, and a host of other innovative programs designed to move the convict from idleness and frustration in a prison facility to monitoring by community programs, where it is expected that rehabilitation can be more successful. Community-based corrections includes building or rebuilding social ties, obtaining employment and education, and securing a place for the offender in the routine functioning of society (Clear and Cole 1986). The development of offender programs by states, counties, and cities has depended increasingly on contracting with private facilities and companies to carry out the intent of community corrections. Political scientist Theodore Lowi states that:

> [The] privatization of corrections which in specific terms of the extant movement towards community corrections, has come to be regarded as service delivery by private agencies on a contractual base. The idea itself could have its roots in current political movements which have arisen out of the more or less universal acceptance of the need for governmental intervention and control of the lives of men coupled with the desire to

control and curtail the burgeoning government authority by entrusting the identification of problem areas, the promulgation of government policy, and the implementation of control measures to private interest groups to embody the will of the people in a free and democratic society. (Jayewardene, Juliana and Talbot 1983, 100)

Empirically speaking, even with the alternatives to incarceration that community programs provide, the current number of prison facilities in the nation cannot handle the escalating growth in numbers of convicts that society has determined need to be incarcerated. According to Department of Corrections officials there are approximately 400 major adult correctional institutions and about 250 major juvenile institutions in the United States.[1] These facilities, many of which were built long ago, are costly to operate and maintain, and cannot handle the increase in convictions occurring in the criminal justice system.

As of December of 1986, thirty-eight states and three territories were under federal court order to relieve overcrowding—a result of many prisons having added second and third bunks and/or floor mattresses to single-occupant cells, to accommodate the rising populations (Carter et al. 1985, 101). Others are being used to provide "fair treatment" and to reduce the "cruel and unusual" punishment of prisoners (Hennessey 1986, 10). As the court has said, "though his rights may be diminished..., a prisoner is not wholly stripped of constitutional protection when he is imprisoned for crime" (*Wolf* v. *McDonnell*, 1974).[2]

In the case of *Bell* v. *Wolfish*, 1979, a Federal District Court found overcrowded conditions unconstitutional (Carter et al. 1985, 101–2). This case was eventually overturned by the U.S. Supreme Court but remains significant in that the lower courts' activist posture toward prison treatment of inmates and the issue of overcrowding had become more blatant.

The American Civil Liberties Union (ACLU) states that the root causes for most prison disturbances, as well as the current crises in corrections, are overcrowded conditions and inhumane treatment of prisoners. The ACLU is involved in litigation in twenty-five states regarding overcrowded conditions (Elvin 1984).

Why are prisons not being built rapidly enough? First, the average cost of a five-hundred-bed prison in 1991 was more than $30 million, and every year there is a shortage of 80,000 to 100,000 cells. Secondly, the average cost of building an average cell has escalated to anywhere from $80,000 to $200,000 (DiPaola 1986; Council of State Governments 1985; Krajick 1982, 22). The average annual cost for the state to house a prisoner in one cell in 1991 was approximately $20,000. Finally, one thousand new inmates enter the prison system, annually (Bivens 1986). Interestingly, construction costs are only 6 per cent of the total cost of the prison over a thirty-year period. A $30 million prison may cost taxpayers over a half billion dollars, most of which is investment interest over the life of the obligation. It has been reported that the next decade will require a growth of prison space costing over $5 billion (Mullen, Chotabor, and Carrow 1985).

There are many who claim that private companies can build, operate, and maintain prisons more cheaply than the government, and continue to provide the same or better level of services while simultaneously decreasing inmate idleness through training, industries and innovative programs.[3] Peter Greenwood, an analyst with the Rand Corporation, states:

> The government is not going to give us better prisons, better programs or better personnel. It has tried but it can't... So it is time to get government out of the prison business. Who could take over? The same people who run other large institutions such as hospitals and colleges. The same people who have developed techniques for serving thousands of meals and for housing travelers. The same people who run most of the job training programs in this Country: Private Industry. (Travis, Latessa and Vito 1985, 25).

Increasing movement by the criminal justice system toward community corrections through contracting for programs and services, the immense cost of building much-needed cell space to relieve overcrowding and accommodate a growing inmate population, and high operation costs, have led to a growing use of the private sector to house prisoners, operate prisons, and be involved in prisoner rehabilitation (Evans 1987; Durham 1988). Chief Justice Warren Burger added momentum to the privatization movement. He stated that "idleness in prison" poisoned rehabilitation efforts and increased the cost of operations. His dream of prisons becoming "factories within fences" is believed to be a way of reducing idleness (Hennessey 1986). Inmate energies could be channeled toward productive endeavors (Farkas 1985). This is interesting too, given the probable growth in numbers of prisoners expected to be confined by the year 2020 (see figure 3.1).

Barbara Auerbach (1972) states that the private sector has the potential for enhancing and expanding prison industries. Twenty states now have legislation approving opening prisons to prison industries. According to Joan Mullen (1985), industries are already involved in the "factories within fences" concept. Prisoners are producing products as diverse as prefabricated housing, data entry components, and photography materials. The expectation is that prisoners will not only be able to work to pay fines and restitution to victims but also be able to contribute to the cost of their keep and prison operations.

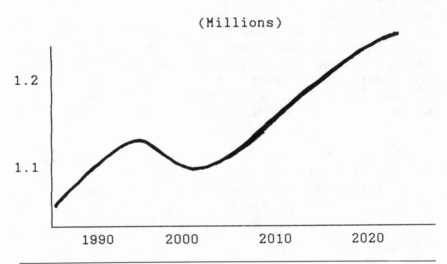

Figure 3.1
Projection of National and State Prison Population Growth

Source: MacDonald, Douglas (ed.), *Private Prisons and the Public Interest* (New Brunswick, N.J.: Rutgers University Press, 1990), p. 9.

Prisons operated by the private sector may be better able to facilitate this effort.

Historical Perspective

Historically, the private sector has had a major role and responsibility in operating prisons.[4] The private sector has been a primary source of change in corrections. Stanley Swart (1982) reports that almost all departures in modern corrections, and historically, have originated outside the "official" circle of the public sector.

As far back as Hammurabi of Babylon, records show that typical punishment for crimes included restitution, exile, and a wide variety of corporal and capital punishments. The principle of law utilized was an eye for an eye, and a tooth for a tooth (Dodge 1975). The workhouse or house of corrections has a much more recent tradition. Having its beginning in 1555 in England, it was related to the idea of poor relief. A tradition of confinement at productive labor as a means of checking vagrancy and other evils was established at these institutions. Anthony Travisono (1984) reports that workhouses were often operated by the private sector. Countries could not afford to operate them or build them. Fees were charged prisoners from their labor rewards. Jailers were not paid salaries. The position of jailer itself was sold from one individual to another (Jayewardene and Talbot 1982). Workhouses were moneymaking operations, sinecures, for officials who had no government funds to run an institution. Jayewardene and Talbot (1982) note that the church also played a prominent role in housing criminals and the poor, using donations as a source of funds.

Until the early seventeenth century, the main punishment choices continued to be corporal, capital, or banishment. In 1682, William Penn planned houses of correction as a major instrument of deterrence and justice (Dodge 1975; McKelvey 1968; Tappan 1951). These detention facilities engendered a major change in punishment from traditional methods such as torture and death, to detainment, work, and penance in order to rehabilitate convicts. In fact, the "Great Law of 1682" specified that "every county within the Province of Pennsylvania and territories there unto belonging shall. . . build or cause to be built a house of restraint, labor and punishment" for persons convicted by law (Dodge 1975). Hartford, Massachusetts in 1699, and Connecticut in 1727, also directed "sturdy beggars" to be locked up at hard labor to pay for their crimes and pay their keep (McKelvey 1968).

Throughout most of the eighteenth century, jails were maintained through a combination of fees and labor sales. The Pennsylvania legislature passed laws requiring the employment of prisoners upon public roads. Orlando Lewis reports that prisoners in Pennsylvania were to meet their expenses through labor (Lewis 1967). In 1787, the Philadelphia Society for Alleviating the Miseries of Public Prisons fostered the idea that punishment should not destroy the offender physically or mentally. In 1790, the Walnut Street Jail was reestablished to include solitary confinement. Inmates were placed in solitary confinement where each convict was expected to be penitent, learn the Scriptures and complete small jobs such as shoemaking, weaving, tailoring, chopping wood, and other jobs that could be done in confinement (McKelvey 1968). Each male prisoner was to be accredited with fair pay for his labor and was debited with the cost of his food, clothes, and lodging.

From the time of the nineteenth century, there were two basic types of prison systems: the Pennsylvania System, which emphasized solitary confinement, work in solitude, and personal penance; and the Auburn System, modeled after the Auburn Prison in New York, which pursued the same three goals except that work was performed by groups of prisoners with no communication or eye contact between them and solitary confinement being reserved for the Sabbath and non-work hours. The Auburn System eventually prevailed in the nineteenth century in America as it was conducive to production methods and helped prisons become self-sufficient (Dodge 1975).

The Newgate Prison in New York, using the Auburn System, in 1802 accrued a surplus of funds by contracting with outside manufacturers to use prison labor to produce various goods. In 1825, Auburn, Wethersfield, Charlestown, and Baltimore prisons were declaring profits from prison contracted labor industries (McKelvey 1968). In 1828, Auburn and other prisons proclaimed themselves self-sufficient (Lewis 1967). The chief product of the New Jersey State prison was nail-making. Proceeds from nails sold by the keeper were used to make the prison self-sufficient (Barnes 1965).

In 1838, the New Jersey legislature passed an act requiring all able-bodied prisoners to be kept at "hard work" and all proceeds from contract labor to be used to offset costs of keep. Each prisoner had a separate account where wages and debits were added and deducted regularly. Between 1841 and 1858 the contract labor method flourished and enriched the coffers of most prisons.

The California legislature passed the Prison Act of 1851, which allowed prisoners to be turned over to contractors who would clothe, feed, and detain them in return for their labor. Escapes, however, were rampant. In one instance, a large contractor reached an agreement with the State of California for his company to build San Quentin Prison and operate it. However, the company soon went bankrupt (Prison Privatization...1986).

The Civil War seriously damaged the prison-labor contract enterprise. Most males were remanded to duty in the Army. Of those remaining, their labor product found no market. The prison-labor contract system never recovered. In 1871 the Virginia Supreme Court ruled that prison labor was no better than slave labor on plantations and in factories and consequently was outlawed (U.S. Congress 1986). In 1877, a report to the New Jersey Legislature observed that prison labor is a threat to free labor. As a result of labor unions lobbying against prison production, many states developed legislation to halt prison manufacturing by restricting types and quantities of products that could be produced. In 1887, Congress passed laws restricting interstate movement of prison-made goods (Tappan 1951).

In 1891, New Jersey abolished contract prison labor. Other states followed suit. Since then, and until the late 1970s, prison industries have had a minimal impact on decreasing the cost of corrections. In the past, the private sector alone had the ability to utilize prisoners' skills and decrease prison operational costs. Advocates now argue that the private sector, through competitive motivation and concern for efficiency and innovation, can once again transform old prisons with idle masses of inmates into productive, cost-efficient operations. It has been further argued that private prison companies can ease the burden of overcrowding by building new prisons in a more timely and cost-efficient manner.

Current literature details the perceived barriers to the privatization of prisons and problems that may occur if the state contracts for prison operations on a large scale. These include a number of political, administrative, financial, legal/constitutional, and social issues that have caused governments to act cautiously on the privatization movement and, in some cases, declare moratoriums (Fenton 1985).

Political Issues

The criminal justice system, now devoid of interest-group support and political advantage, may use the experience of organized businesses' involvement in prisons to feather their nest. Prison-business interest groups may lobby for longer sentences, stronger penalties, stringent parole standards, or attempt to redirect social policy like "deinstitutionalization," so as to gain from higher prison numbers.[5]

"Opponents [to privatization] contend that private prison operators will exert an untoward influence on criminal justice policy and contribute to the incarceration of more prisoners under worse conditions. Some people believe that prison expansion programs resemble supply side economic polices in that increases in the supply of prison cells produce additional prisoners to fill them" (Ring 1987, 12). Ira Robbins (1986) also suggests that companies might, through advertising, attempt to make society more conscious of crime so as to instill fear in the population, which would result in more stiff sentencing, decreased alternative sentencing, and a higher prison population.

Another important political issue is that the private-sector building of prisons could be used to circumvent the voters when bond referenda fail, which translates to less democratic control and a less accountable governing body (Pennsylvania State Legislature 1985; Council of State Governments 1985). On the other hand, should governments have a monopoly in certain services? Fitzgerald asserts, "Natural monopoly conditions are said to exist in many service areas, such as the municipal provision of electricity or water "(Fitzgerald 1988, 88). The Government usually assumes the role of provider in these areas, ostensibly, to protect the public from price gouging and to prevent wasteful duplication of effort. Even if one accepts this as necessary, benefits of competition can still be achieved if government will establish franchises—exclusive service provisions—and require bid competitions by private firms to operate them. In this way some of the benefits of competitive enterprise could be obtained by placing government in the role of bargaining agent for customers in the franchise area.

Administrative Issues

The question has arisen as to whether the public would continue to have access to prisons and prison records, or would there instead be closed meetings and record-hiding as in private industry today (Geis 1987; Robbins 1986). Gilbert Geis and Ira Robbins have said in this regard that the secrecy that surrounds private company records and plans would be an intolerable interference for governments contracting for prison management.

A second major issue is whether the cost-effectiveness of prison privatization is a form of union busting and exploitation of labor, with lower wages, lower pensions, and less employee benefits. There is resistance from government employee groups and government managers regarding private operations, as they believe that companies hire fewer people, decrease employee forces, and reduce training time.[6] Stephen Moore (1987, 69) argues, however, that few, if any, public employees lose jobs as a result of privatization. Employees, he says, are placed in other government positions. He also found that losses in unemployment benefits and welfare are negligible compared to the benefits and welfare are negligible compared to the benefits of privatization. My own visits to three privately-operated facilities during this study indicated that two facilities had originally been public prisons. No public employees were displaced. Butler County Prison chose to keep the unionized guard force. The operators of the Hamilton County Prison offered all original county employees their same positions, without reduction in pay.[7]

A third major issue is whether private entrepreneurs would engage in uncontrollable cost-cutting activities, design shortcuts, a reduction in safety standards, and an increase in corner-cutting methods, which would result in inhumane and unsafe conditions. Corner "cost" cutting has been refuted by several studies performed on contracted municipal services. A 1984 nationwide study completed by the Department of Housing and Urban Development (Ecodata) found that "for many of the services [studied], the individual cities with the lowest cost of service delivery also achieved among the highest levels of service quality" (Moore 1987, 67–68). Also, an earlier 1981 study performed by the California Tax Foundation observed that of all the cities studied, twice as many cities indicated that services improved when contracting out for those same services rather than having declined or remained the same.

A fourth major question is whether in a attempt to save money, private companies may attempt to "skim the cream" of prisoners by contracting for housing only the low security, problem-free inmates, leaving the higher cost hardcore criminals for government to house (Anderson 1985; Mullen, Chotabor, and Carrow 1985; Patrick 1986).

Other administrative issues include questions of what will happen in case of strikes, bankruptcy, or emergency situations. Obviously contingency plans would have to be developed and agreed on before a contract is approved. Should employees strike, shutting down operations, or a company declare itself no longer able to fiscally operate, or should a state of emergency develop, plans would need to be available for a temporary government takeover, the locating of a second vendor, or for finding adequate temporary facilities within short time frames and with no break in service (Robbins 1986; Cullen 1986).

Lawrence Finley states that:

One of the primary concerns of any government unit that is considering the privatization of government service is ensuring delivery of the service by the private company. It is therefore imperative that the financial soundness of a company be established early in the bidding process. Legal counsel would be well advised to spell out the financial requirements of the government unit before a contract or franchise will be entered into. The government unit may satisfy itself by bonding requirements, review of financial statements and balance sheets, and requiring personal guarantees. Yet, no matter how careful a government unit is in selecting a financially sound private company, there may come a day when the private contractor is unable or unwilling to perform according to the terms of the contract. (Finley 1989, 144)

Financial Issues

A major financial issue is whether private companies operating prisons would be more efficient. Certainly the profit and loss incentives of private companies differ greatly from the budget-building incentives of bureaucracy. It is, however, in an owner's interest to save on costs wherever and whenever possible (Geis 1987; Robbins 1986; Council of State Governments 1985). For example the Immigration and Naturalization Service (INS) was paying up to $80 a day for illegal aliens housed in country jails. Now, INS pays $20 a day to private operators on a contract basis (Mullen 1985).

A second financial issue is whether private prison operating costs may be lower in the short run but eventually increase to the same level or more than public sector operations. Would privatization of prisons have a tendency toward oligopoly or monopoly? Would costs rise and would it be difficult to dislodge that company when it submits its inflated budget at contract renewal time?

Supporters of prison privatization argue that during a contract period of three, five, or ten years, costs to a contractor would be fixed. Companies unable to maintain cost levels or unable to produce profit through efficiency and accountability would go out of business (Logan 1985). The possibility of low bidding could be counteracted by longer contracts. It has been suggested by Gilbert Geis (1987) that government would still be saddled with the costs of monitoring private operations and that monitoring is a hidden cost that must be recognized in the calculation of all costs. However, the monitoring of public sector facilities is usually performed by an outside oversight agency, the cost of which is not normally calculated in the public sector cost of operation, either. One would expect monitoring costs to be nearly the same whether the facility is public or private.

A financial issue not often mentioned but having great impact on the future is that society will eventually have to reckon with the huge government pension system growing up around us. Taxpayers pay most of the contribution for state and local government employee pensions. "The unfunded liability of state pension debt has been estimated at more than $1,000 for every American adult. New York City has a liability exceeding $3 billion and Boston has a pension liability in excess of $1.2 billion, representing nearly $2000 in pension debt for every citizen of that city" (Fitzgerald 1988, 87). Privatizing prisons will reduce public pension indebtedness. Private Pension Systems will take up the slack.

Legal/Constitutional Issues

There are several major legal concerns foundational to the ability of private sector companies to operate prisons. The first issue has to do with whether the delegation of this state function is constitutional. The U.S. Constitution provides that all legislative power is vested in the Congress of the United States. Due to social complexities, changes, advances, and administrative realities, this doctrine has not been strictly adhered to, allowing the development and oversight of many policies and regulations to be delegated to other entities (for example, regulatory agencies). Thus, Congress, under the "necessary and proper" clause of the Constitution, can delegate authority sufficient to effectuate its purposes. Even in areas that have traditionally been thought of as "belonging" to the public sector rather than private sector, courts have tolerated broad delegation of lawmaking power to private bodies (Robbins 1986). Some states including Florida,

Michigan, New Mexico, Tennessee, and Texas, have enacted specific legislation for the private operation of prisons.[8]

Importantly, the federal courts have already ruled on the constitutionality of prison privatization. In *Medina* v. *O'Neill*, 1982, the U.S. District Court ruled that although the private Immigration and Naturalization Service (INS) facility operator, Danner Inc., was just as liable as the Federal Government for abuses against prisoners, the INS "did have the constitutional right" to contract with private groups for detention of aliens.[9] Indeed, the Court explicitly reflected the counterargument at several places in the decision. Additionally, Norman Carlson argues that federal corrections agencies have the legal authority to contract for the management of entire facilities under 18 U.S.C. 4082 which allows the Attorney General to designate as a place of confinement "any facility, whether maintained by the Federal Government of otherwise..." (Carlson 1986, 3).

A second constitutional issue is whether the acts of private prison operators constitute "state" acts in terms of liability; that is, whether all alleged infringement of rights would be fairly attributable to the state. State action has been generally determined by three tests: the public function test, the close-nexus test, and the state compulsion test (Robbins 1986; Cullen 1986; Johnson 1986).

First the United States Supreme Court, through the public function test, has determined that state action exists when a state delegates to private parties power traditionally and exclusively reserved to the state. Secondly, in *Milonas* v. *Williams*, 1983, the court provided for the close-nexus test for state action stating that the question is "whether there is a sufficient close nexus between the state and the challenged action...so that the action of the latter may be fairly treated as that of the state itself." In this case, because the state so situated itself with the private entity as to be considered a joint participant in the offending actions, the private operator could be looked upon as performing state actions. Thirdly, the state compulsion test, as discussed in *Lombard* v. *Eunice Kennedy Shriver Center*, 1983, provides that a private operator's actions can be considered state actions when the plaintiff was compelled, though circumstances of institutionalization, to utilize the services of the private operator.[10]

A third constitutional issue has to do with the trade-off private vendors must make between efficiency (saving money) and the Fifth/Fourteenth Amendments to the Constitution regarding due process, as well as the Eighth Amendment, which prohibits "cruel and unusual punishment" of prisoners. A private operator's chief concern is economy and profit margins. Any safeguards required of the private company to ensure procedural due process, i.e. methods available to prisoners to ensure fair treatment and substantive due process (for example, that prisoners be treated with a minimum degree of fairness), would cost money and decrease company profits. Additionally, under the Eighth Amendment, private companies would have to provide benefits, programs, and activities enough to ensure that prisoners have adequate living conditions, medical care, and the necessities of life. The larger the scope of programs and benefits required by the government of the private company, the less profitable the private prison would likely become (Durham 1986, 1482–83).

Charles Logan states:

Contracting, in conjunction with governmental monitoring, adds a new layer of independent review of correctional decisions and actions, thus improving due process. Contracting can help clarify the purposes of imprisonment and the rules and procedures that define due process. Contracting for operating prisons is compatible with federal law and the laws of many states; specific enabling legislation has been passed in some states. (Logan 1990, 41)

A fourth legal issue has to do with whether the use of restraint, force, and deadly force can be delegated by the state to the private sector. Connie Mayer (1986) argues that, "the power is inherent in the state to prescribe, within limits of state and federal constitutions, reasonable regulations necessary to preserve the public order, health, safety and morals." Mayer argues further that police power is a power of states, to regulate as they will.[11]

Joan Mullen (1985) states that counties are deputizing private company guards and providing them with defined responsibilities in their contracts. One study notes that some states have no legal designation for private company guards, whereas some government guards are given "peace officer" status or are deputized ("Pennsylvania State Legislature 1985).

A fifth legal issue is: Who is liable for improper treatment or abuse of prisoners? Opponents of prison privatization argue that the state cannot void its responsibility for liability by contracting with a private company (Mayer 1986; Robbins 1986; Mullen 1985; Hornblum 1985). A prisoner may file suit under 42 U.S.C.A. 1983, which means the state could be liable, and so, government cannot shift its responsibility though contracting to private companies.[12] As the U.S. District Court said in *Medina* v. *O'Neill*, 1982, the holding of prisoners is a state action under the "state function" test. In this instance, both the Danner Company and the Federal Government were held liable (Hornblum 1985). However, supporters of prison privatization argue that state liability, now shared with the private company, would decrease overall state liability costs. They say insurance provided by private companies could protect companies against lawsuits. Moreover, contract requirements and adherence to accreditation guidelines could limit liability suits (Robbins 1986; Logan 1990, 187).

Lawrence Finley asks: "What duty does a government unit owe when it grants a private contract for the performance of a public service? In general, a governmental unit has a duty to comply with all procedural requirements as outlined previously." In addition, and more important in terms of tort liability, a government unit has a duty to investigate and examine the qualifications of the private company with whom it seeks to do business (Finley 1989, 143–44).[13]

A sixth issue is that of parole hearings. Most criminal justice researchers agree that parole decisionmaking and decisions affecting "good time", as well as discipline hearings that affect good time, cannot be delegated to private prison management (Geis 1987; Mayer 1986). The risk of bias, they say, is too great to allow private prison officials to participate in decisionmaking that impacts on prisoners' lengths of stay in the prison. Gilbert Geis (1987, 94) argues, however, that these decision-making processes could easily be arbitrated by an outside "official" arbiter or parole agent.

Closely related to the parole issue is the question of the development of "prison rules." All prisons have rules by which inmates are expected to proceed, the violation of which impacts upon "good time" and may then prolong a convict's length of prison stay. Prisons view rules as a method to reduce liability claims by limiting hazards of prison life and by enhancing the safety of correctional officers and inmates. If rules are too general or unclear they infringe upon the "due process" clause of the Fifth and Fourteenth Amendments. If the rules are too restrictive, they may create hardship and infringe upon the "cruel and unusual punishment" aspect of the Eighth Amendment (Durham 1986). Prison rulemaking would, of course, encounter difficulties with the private sector just as it does in the public sector.

Charles Ring states:

Many of the disciplinary offenses that can result in major or minor sanctions leave little room for arbitrary or subjective enforcement. A partial list includes: (1) escape or possession of escape tools, (2) refusal to take a breathalizer test or to provide a urine sample, (3) possession, manufacture or introduction of a gun, firearm, explosive, ammunition, weapon, sharpened instrument, knife or tool, (4) fighting with, assaulting, or threatening another person, and (5) killing. Other offenses, however, permit a great deal of discretionary or arbitrary enforcement. These include: (1) disobeying an order, lying to, or insolence toward a staff member, (2) failure to keep one's person or one's quarters in accordance with institutional rules, (3) being out of place, (4) inexcusable absence from, willful failure to properly perform, or refusal to accept a work or program assignment, and (5) conduct which interferes with the security or orderly running of an institution. (Ring 1987, 19)

Social Issues

The first social issue has to do with whether offenders are kept in prisons for the entire duration of their sentences. Non-incarceration as well as early release, early parole, plea bargaining, sentence reduction, early community "reintegration," and other such programs have been implemented because of overcrowed conditions and the high cost of imprisonment. It is argued that privatization of prisons would fortify the justice system since prison costs would be reduced and more cell space would be available. Longer prison stays they say would be an inducement toward decreasing crime (Logan 1985; Logan and Rausch 1985). Obviously, society would need to rethink the value of non-incarceration and early release programs.

Secondly, there is a "symbolism" factor that is lost when private firms begin to enforce public rules and regulations. Mick Ryan states that organizations like the American Civil Liberties Union (ACLU) and the American Bar Association (ABA) are

> ...particularly concerned with what they term the 'symbolic issue' and its practical consequences. The argument here is that to give up to the private sector what is traditionally taken to be a state function could seriously undermine the legitimacy and authority of those exercising that function, a serious concern which it has posed somewhat ironically by asking, 'Does it weaken that authority, however—as well as the integrity of a system of justice—when an inmate looks at this keeper's uniform and, instead of encountering an emblem that reads 'Federal Bureau of Prisons' or 'State Department of Corrections', he faces one that says 'Acme Corrections Company'?" (Ryan and Ward 1989, 39)

Privatization embraces justice because prison supply becomes "more responsive to changes in demand, both upward and downward" (Logan 1990).

Three additional issues that especially concern opponents of prison privatization are the possibility of retaliation against inmates, the provision of unethical therapies, and the possibility of corruption and graft. The first argument is that private companies may be inclined to retaliate against prisoners who "make waves" by threatening to transfer them to less suitable prisons. The second argument is that as private prisons of necessity would have to depend upon large numbers of inmates for revenues, there exists some possibility that unethical, abusive, or unfair therapies or practices could be imposed upon prisoners in order to extend their sentences or cause them to break rules and lose good time. Here, again, continuous oversight by the public sector and the development of a third party grievance process could help to decrease the possibility of victimization of convicts.

Graft and corruption within a private prison would be difficult to ensure against, as it is with publicly-managed prisons. According to Randall Fitzgerald (1988, 82), "some critics fear that to expand profits, contracting companies will routinely resort to bribery, kickbacks, payoffs, bid-rigging and other questionable practices."

Endorsing and Dissenting Groups

Given the issues discussed above, different groups have come out for or against prison privatization. The American Correction Association and the National Governor's Association have endorsed the concept of privatization of prisons (Gest 1984; Donahue 1989). At the National Governor's convention, New York Governor Mario Cuomo said, "It is not government's obligation to provide [produce] services but to see that they are provided" (Tolchin 1985, A26). According to Martin Tolchin (1985), a number of governors agreed that private companies do a better job in providing correction services because they are free from the drawbacks of bureaucracy.

The President's Commission of Privatization declared in 1988 that contracting "appears to be an effective method for the management and operation of prisons and jails at any level of government" (Donahue 1989, 155). However, several groups at the Congressional House Privatization Hearings in Washington made arguments against the privatization of prisons. The American Civil Liberties Union (ACLU) staff lawyer and representative Edwin I. Koren stated that private companies could never be as responsible for inmate well-being as governments are. The President of the American Federation of Government Employees, David Kelly, stated that lower costs means less personnel, which translates to escapes and inhumane conditions. Gerald McEntree, President of American Federation of State, County and Municipal Employees, stated that he does not believe privatization of prisons is in the best interest of prisoners, the public, or public employees as there are too many legal, political, and ethical questions involved. Wayne Huggins, President of the National Sheriffs Association stated that the Association is against the idea; however, sheriffs in counties throughout the nation are looking at all alternatives to reduce idleness, recidivism, and overcrowding.[14]

Additionally, Mark Cunniff, Director of the National Association of Criminal Justice Planners, asked: "Should justice be a profit making enterprise? Should it be an industry that manufactures a consumer product? We are talking about taking away people's liberty and I have real questions about the proprietary of anyone but the state doing that" (Krajick 1984, 13). Finally, Charles Ring states that:

> The American Bar Association (ABA) is concerned about the prospect of private prisons. At its 1986 mid-year meeting, the ABA adopted a resolution urging 'that jurisdictions that are considering the privatization of prisons and jails not proceed to so contract until the complex constitutional, statutory, and contractual issues are satisfactorily developed and resolved'. The resolution defines privatization as referring to 'contracting for total operational responsibility for prison or jail'. The definition excepts contracting for food preparation, medical care, and other institutional services or for operation of 'non-secure facilities such as half-way houses'. A motion to amend the resolution by substituting the language 'proceed only with great caution' for 'not proceed' was defeated 143 to 128. (Ring 1987, 7)

Barriers to Entry

What then are the real (as opposed to perceived) barriers to entering the private prison market? What has prevented private companies from contracting for operations of prisons?

In Pennsylvania, the Buckingham Security Company purchased land and proposed to build a 750-cell protective custody prison in the western part of the state. In early 1985, legislation prompted by the research work performed by the Pennsylvania State Legislative Budget and Finance Committee, and resulting from public and official pressure for alternatives to prison overcrowding, was developed and on its way to what seemed easy passage (Hornblum 1985). Very quickly, however, lobbying forces including the American Civil Liberties Union (ACLU), American Federation of State, County and Municipal Employees (AFSCME), and the Pennsylvania Prison Society introduced an opposing bill that would place a moratorium on new private prison operations in the state. This was the Pennsylvania Private Prison Moratorium and Study Act, passed in late 1986. It has led to the loss of a dream for several private companies interested in prison management and the loss of needed cell space for the State of Pennsylvania. The main concern that led to a moratorium on new private prison operations was voiced by Jack Case, a director of a community service project for the Pennsylvania Prison Society. He states that "eighty percent of prison management costs are due to personnel. Therefore, if [private companies] cutback on guards, teachers, social workers and medical staff, [they] will be less economically burdened and [be able to] increase [their] profits" (Hornblum 1985, 28). This could, he said, result in inhumane and unfair treatment of prisoners. The ACLU spokesperson echoed this concern stating, "If making profit is the corporation's prime goal, it will be accomplished to the detriment of prisoners" (Hornblum 1985, 25). The most often alluded-to barrier to entry then is the fear that the level and quality of treatment and attention that privately-operated prisons would provide to prisoners would be diminished.

A second frequently-discussed barrier is that liability insurance rates would be very high. Recent prison vendors in Kentucky and New Mexico had to terminate negotiations to operate prisons because they could not obtain a high enough level of insurance. Danner Company, the defendant in the *Medina* v. *O'Neill* case went out of business as a result of a liability conviction (Robbins 1986, 358). Although the state may not be able to void its responsibility of liability, its sharing of liability responsibility with the private operator would add a substantial cost to private prison operations.[15]

A third major barrier to the development of private prisons has to do with local governing officials' fears that contracting with a private company to build and operate a facility will be construed as circumvention of public decision-making by referenda. A company that takes over operation of an existing prison facility does not risk this sentiment, but most private prison negotiations include supplying both facilities (cell space) and operational management. Public officials are very sensitive to public opinion and are reluctant to risk being associated with projects that might prove to be publicly disquieting.

A fourth barrier to the use of private prisons is the question of the constitutionality of delegating the state function of imprisonment to private individuals or companies. As stated earlier in this chapter, some state and county jurisdictions have developed laws authorizing the private operation of prison facilities (Durham 1986). However, most states do not have legislation authorizing private operations; indeed, some have specific rules against it. Private companies often wave negotiating in states where the constitutionality question is under debate. These states lose the availability of an alternative method of incarceration to reduce overcrowding.

A fifth barrier is the question of the propriety of a state delegating the police power of using deadly force and restraint. Mayer indicates that in *Sinnot* v. *Davenport*, 1959, the U.S. Supreme Court held that police power is kept by the state under the Tenth Amendment and that state legislatures generally delegate police power to political subdivisions and not to private individuals and companies. On the other hand, Mayer cites the U.S. Supreme Court's decision in *Estates Planning Corporation* v. *Commissioner*, 1939, to support claims that the state can contract with private institutions to provide police power (Mayer 1986). Mayer goes on to suggest the enabling legislation at the federal and state levels could provide language to legitimize even more securely the contracting of police powers.

A sixth barrier to the privatization of prisons is the overcoming of concern for the management of parole and discipline decisions. Clearly the private prison managers having input into parole and discipline decisions risk a conflict of interests between business profit motives and the need to release prisoners when they should be released (Mayer 1986; Robbins 1986). In most cases no standards or procedures exist for the private operator to follow to guide his relationship with the criminal justice authorities such as parole boards, probation departments, and halfway houses. Moreover, mechanisms do not exist for intervention by an outside parole agent or third party to make discipline and "good time" decisions. This barrier could be overcome by agreed-upon standards and the appointment of a third-party discipline adjudication agent.

A seventh barrier to the use of private prisons is that no standards exist for the operation and management of a prisoner for the training of prison personnel (Robbins 1986; Mullen 1985; Anderson 1985). Many jurisdictions are reluctant to contract out the operation of jails or prisons to private companies because they have no set standards against which to monitor operations and prisoner treatment. Most county jails, having been operated by the sheriff or police chief, have operated with traditional management practices and locally-issued regulations and policies. With the probability of having to share liability responsibility with a private company, standards would need to be outlined in contracts, in very explicit terms; otherwise the jurisdiction could not hold the company accountable in the strictest sense.

Chapter four includes a comparison between private and public operators' comments regarding the above-stated barriers to market entry and other significant barriers. Information is included in chapter four which explains how currently-operating private companies have overcome these barriers and what impact their methods have had upon costs and operations.

The Emergence of Private Prisons

Although significant barriers exist to entry into the private prison market by new companies as stated above, a number of companies are already involved in this new industry, and the potential for continued growth exists. Durham states that "indeed, that role does appear likely to expand in the near future" (Durham 1988; Fenton 1985; Lee and Wollan 1985; Logan and Raush 1985). But to better understand why the management of a large maximum-security prison has not yet been contracted out to a private company, one must understand the differences between jails and prisons, and levels of security among prisons. Jails and prisons are the two main places where prisoners are incarcerated. These are supplemented by detention centers, which are established for holding prisoners a short time. Centers such as the federal Immigration and Naturalization Service (INS) facilities are considered detention centers. This last group, more than prisons and jails, are managed by private companies.

Jails hold people awaiting trial, prisoners sentenced for relatively minor offenses (a year or less), convicts awaiting transport to state and federal prisons, and the spillover of convicts for whom space is not available at state prisons (Geis 1987). Virtually all counties in the nation have a jail. Jails, given the range of types of convicts and variety of sentences imposed, are usually maximum security, full lock-up facilities, with armed guards.

Prisons are state- and federal-level facilities that hold serious offenders and felons. These convicts serve longer sentences, including life sentences. Provisions for carrying out the death penalty are in place at state and federal prisons. State prisons are usually maximum security facilities, but can be of other security levels depending on the type of convicts housed there (Clear and Cole 1986). Federal prisons may be minimum or maximum security.

Maximum security prisons house 52 per cent of all state prisoners. They were built to prevent escapes and to deter dangerous prisoners from harming guards or one another. Medium security prisons are externally similar to maximum security prisons. However, prisoners are perceived to be less dangerous and generally have more freedom of movement, more privileges, and more contact with the outside world. Medium security prisons house 37 per cent of all state prisoners (Clear and Cole 1986). These prisoners are not considered intractable, hardened criminals. The remaining 11 per cent of state prisoners are housed in minimum security facilities. These are the least violent offenders, many of whom are white collar workers who live in dormitory-style facilites and are given the opportunity of involvement in many rehabilitation and work-release programs.

The number of women prisoners in any one state is so small that usually they are housed in one state facility. Juveniles, unless considered extremely dangerous, are mostly housed in minimum or medium security facilities.

The Federal Bureau of Prisons is responsible for holding convicted federal offenders, material witness, and aliens convicted of federal offenses. The U.S. Immigration and Naturalization Service (INS) is responsible for detaining illegal aliens awaiting deportation from the United States.

As stated earlier, all the various levels of prisons, jails, and detention centers are experiencing overcrowding. Over the last ten years, private companies have emerged to operate prisons, jails, and detention centers, and have helped to decrease prison overcrowding. According to the Director of the Reason Foundation's Local Government Center, Phillip E. Fixler:

> Private companies have proven their capabilities by first providing housekeeping and support services, such as prisoner medical care and transport, then progressing to halfway houses, detention centers, and now accepting responsibility for operating high security facilities, and soon prisons themselves. It would be unfortunate, indeed, if unprogressive forces of the status quo were able to arrest the privatization solution. (Geis 1987, 95)

Senator Arlen Spector of Pennsylvania has called private corrections "the major unexamined new social policy of the 1990s" (Geis 1987, 96).

The first privately-operated secure correctional institution was the Weaversville Intensive Treatment Unit, built in Northampton, Pennsylvania—a twenty-bed high-security dormitory-style training facility for delinquents. It was opened in 1976 and operated by RCA. The second privately-operated secure facility was the Okeechobee School for Boys, built in Okeechobee, Florida, and operated since 1982 by the Eckerd Foundation (Eckerd Drugs). A list of private companies that have contracted with various jurisdictions to operate prison facilities has been compiled in table 3.1.[16]

In chapter 4, a cost comparison is made of similar public and private facilities, including a detailed evaluation of each facility's operational programs. In this way, general costs between public and private facilities can be compared in light of the services available, identifying as many "hidden costs" as possible. If a county prison, with an average of 100 inmates per day having a cost of $30 per day per inmate, is compared to a private prison that costs taxpayers significantly more or less per inmate per day but provides nearly the same type, quantity, and level of programs, then more credible arguments can be made regarding the private sector's capacity to operate a prison or jail and that it is either beneficial to the public sector or more costly than its utilization is worth.

Table 3.1
Privately Contracted Penal Facilities

Company	Facilities	First Contract
Associated Marine Institutes	Biscayne Bay Institution Biscayne Bay, Florida State of Florida	1985
	Astro-Park Juvenile Facility Miami, Florida State of Florida	1987
Behavioral Systems Southwest	Delongpre Los Angeles, California INS	1983
	Aurora Detention Center Aurora, Colorado INS	INS
	Pasadena Immigrant Holding Facility Pasadena, California	
	12 other detention facilities	
Buckingham Security Ltd.	Butler County Prison Butler, Pennsylvania	1986 [closed 1989]
Catholic Communications Services	U.S. Marshall Service San Diego, California USMS	1987
Correction Corporation of America	Fayetteville Detention Center, Fayetteville, N.C. FBP	1986
	Laredo Detention Center Laredo, Texas INS	1985
	INS Detention Centers Houston, Texas INS	1985

Company	Facilities	First Contract
	Tall Trees Shelby County Memphis, Tennessee	1985
	Sante Fe Jail Sante Fe, New Mexico	1986
	Silverdale Correct. Center Chattenooga, Tennessee Hamilton County, Tennessee	1984
	Bay County Jail Bay County, Florida	1985
	Grants Jail Grants, New Mexico	1989
	Venus Texas Jail Venus, Texas	
	Cleveland Texas Jail Cleveland, Texas	
Eckerd Foundation	Okeechobee Training School Okeechobee, Florida State of Florida	1982
Eclectic Communications Inc.	Hidden Valley Ranch La Honda, California FBP	1985
	San Mateo, California FBP	
	San Mateo Center	1983
	El Centro Detention Center El Centro, California INS	1986
	US Marshall's Detention Center Los Angeles, California USMS	1987
	Baker California Center Baker, California	

Company	Facilities	First Contract
	Live Oaks Center Live Oaks, California	

Management and
  Training Corporation
	thirteen other facilities
	Eagle Mountain,
	  California
	Artesian Oaks Facility
	Saugus, California	

National Correctional
  Management Inc.
	Three county jails in
	  New Mexico	

NOW Concepts, Inc.	Marion Adjustment Center Louisville, Kentucky	1986

Palo Duro Private
  Detention Services
	Palo Duro Adult
	  Facility
	Palo Duro, California
	FBP
		1984

Pricor Corporation	Houston Pre-Parole Center Houston, Texas State of Texas	1987
	Sweetwater Detention Center Sweetwater, Texas	
	Tuscaloosa Center Tuscaloosa, Alabama	
	Green County Jail Greenville, Tennessee	

RCA/General Electric	Weaversville Intensive
	  Treatment Unit
	Northampton,
	  Pennsylvania
	State of Pennsylvania
		1976

Volunteers of America	St. Paul Facility St. Paul, Minnesota FBP	1985
Wackenhut Services Inc.	Aurora Women's Aurora, Colorado INS	1986

Company	Facilities	First Contract
	Tulsa Training Center Tulsa, Oklahoma	1986
	Mcfarland, California	1989
	Allen Parish, Louisiana	1990
	Kyle Texas Prison State of Texas	

Other companies in private prison business:

American Correctional Systems   Concepts Inc.
Detention Centers of America   Emerson Private Prisons
Gary White and Associates   Operational Support Services
U.S. Corrections Corporation   VIP Company

INS   = Immigration and Naturalization Service
USMS = United States Marshall's Service
FBP   = Federal Bureau of Prisons

Sources: Data compiled from on-site interviews, telephone discussions and various documents (see note 16).

4

Comparison of Private and Public Prison Programs, Costs, and Facilities

Why is the subject of the "costs" of privatization of prisons so important? The quantity of government-provided services and their proportion to total national income (GNP) is greater now than ever before (see table 1.1). Various studies of the privatization of services indicate real and substantial cost savings when governments opt to contract out (see table 2.8). If privately-operated prisons can operate at the same or lower overall costs as public facilities, then cost should not be a reason to reject the attempt by the private sector to enter a market dominated by the public sector.

There has been an increasing tendency by the public prison sector toward contracting for services of all types, including "literally every aspect of institutional corrections" (Camp and Camp 1984, 4; Logan and Rausch 1985). In 1984, fifty agencies reported about $200 million in savings and twenty-two large agency contracts alone were reported to have saved $9.5 million (Camp and Camp 1984). As the public sector depends more and more on contracting out to reduce government expenditures, it is logical to believe that contracting out the entire operation of a public prison or jail could be even more cost effective. In order to determine the cost-efficiency of contracting out for the operation of private prisons, interested parties from the criminal justice system have been calling for the performance of comparative cost studies of similar public and private operated facilities, studies like the National Institute of Corrections' research on the Okeechokee School in Florida, completed in 1985 (Carlson 1986, 7). The NIC report attempted to compare the operation of the Okeechobee School for Boys with the school's own status prior to being operated by the Eckerd Drug Foundation. The study also attempted to compare the operation of Okeechokee with a "similar" Florida facility called Dozier School for Boys. As compared to itself under public management, the study found that more services were available to inmates and that current programs and services had expanded. However, when compared to the Dozier School, the study found the Dozier School to be handling inmates better with less incidents of aggression. Also, the Dozier School had more to offer inmates in terms of education, athletics, and other services at a lower cost than Okeechokee. The Okeechokee study is problematic for two reasons. First, the researchers were not on-site before Eckerd Foundation took over the facility and could not make an adequate comparison. Second, Eckerd is a non-profit foundation. No assurances exist that the normal motives for seeking efficiency are operative when a non-profit organization is managing a facility.

Cost Analysis

A good comparative cost-efficiency analysis should make use of the same cost elements and include all costs in maintaining prisoners (Camp and Camp 1985, 1). Costs that are considered "hidden" or invisible regardless of what sector is operating the facility should be identified. Also, many costs are allocated to another agency budget (Camp and Camp 1985). For instance, transportation of convicts may be allocated to the Sheriff's Department in one facility but not allocated to the Sheriff's Department in the other facility. Fringe benefits for one facility may be allocated to same other state or county budget area but counted in the budget of a second facility (Hatry 1979; Camp and Camp 1985). Efficiency occurs when the quality or quantity of services provided improves with no increase in cost. This implies a need to measure "effectiveness" in some sense (Hatry 1979). To compare the efficiency of prisons will mean ensuring to some degree that the same programs or benefits are available to both prison populations being compared. If two prisons have the same quantity, type and level of prison services available and yet one prison is operating at lower cost than the second, we will consider the first prison to be more "efficient." If the first prison is operating at the same level of costs as a second prison, we will consider them equally efficient (or the first facility to be "just as" efficient as the second).

Most cost analyses of prisons depend upon the use of a "cost-per-prisoner" figure. This figure can be calculated or used incorrectly in prison facility comparisons. It is important that cost-per-prisoner figures be accurate and inclusive (Hatry 1979; McDonald 1990). The figures used to determine cost-per-prisoner are, in this study, the average annual inmate population and the facility's expenditures for given fiscal years. An attempt will be made to identify similar cost elements for the same expenditure categories (Turnbull and Witte 1981; Wayson 1981; Witte 1981; Steelman 1984).

George and Camille Camp (1984) report that most prison and jail facilities do not report all their costs in their report of total annual expenditures. Some funds expended on the care and treatment of inmates are reported by sister agencies. Also, prisons do not usually include the costs of construction in the expenditure totals. Hence, real annual costs are somewhat higher than reported cost expenditures as explained by the Camps in their analysis of prison costs. However, since this study compares very similar facilities that are operating within like levels of government jurisdictions, we will assume unreported costs are similar if not the same for each comparison combination.

Costs and Programs Compared

During the data gathering phase of this study, three privately operated correctional facilities and three publicly operated correctional facilities were visited. Only three of each kind of institution was chosen because the universe of reviewable privately-operated facilities is rather small. After gaining agreements to participate in the study from three private facilities, I enlisted the help of the New Jersey Department of Corrections and the Pennsylvania Department of Public Welfare in locating similar public facilities that would agree to participate in this study.[1] The criteria used to select similar public faciles included size, location, structure, facility age and type, inmate-rated capacity, average daily occupancy, and management style. *Size* included the building dimensions, number of floors, security components, and general layout. *Location* included whether the facility was situated in an urban inner city, city outskirts, or rural setting, whether near transportation routes or accessible to public transportation and airport facilities, and the geographic relationship of these facilities to the oversight authority. Structure type, as a criterion, focuses upon the way buildings were situated to one another and how inmate monitoring is performed.[2] As Charles Logan explains,

> Researchers who compare institutions must face the fact that facilities vary widely on a great many factors that affect costs; so much so that most simple comparisons of per-day rates are not very meaningful. Region or location of a facility affects wage rates, property values, construction costs, and the price of food, fuel, utilities and many other costs. The age of a facility affects maintenance, depreciation, and costs related to efficiency of design. If buildings are still being financed, the speed at which the debt is being retired has a substantial impact on per diem costs, just as housing costs vary by length of mortgage. Construction costs and the purchase or rental of land may be included in some budgets or per diem figures and not in others. (Logan 1990, 96–97)

Each of these criteria may have an impact on costs. Any difference in structure or size may mean a cost advantage of one facility over the other. Urban-situated facilities may have environmental factors that impact costs differently than rural-situated facilities. Capacity and occupancy figures allow this study to examine the impact of overcrowding. The operator's management style as well as the prevailing prison philosophy may impact on cost decisions and program effectiveness.

The three private correctional facilities evaluated were (1) RCA's Weaversville Intensive Treatment Unit, Northampton, Pennsylvania, (2) Correction Corporation of America's (CCA') Silverdale Detention Center, Chattanooga, Tennessee, and (3) Buckingham Security Ltd.'s Butler County Prison, Butler, Pennsylvania. The three public correctional facilities evaluated were (1) Pennsylvania Department of Public Welfare's North Central Secure Treatment Unit, Danville, Pennsylvania, (2) Warren County, New Jersey's Warren County Correctional Center, and (3) Salem County, New Jersey's Salem County Jail.

The on-site visits consisted of structured interview with principal actors (wardens, managers, et cetera), interviews with guards and other staff (for example, chaplains, administrative specialists, nurses) and a tour of the facility. The structured interviews focused on questions of privatization, barriers to privatization, programs available, program goals, cost elements, and other pertinent information (see the sample questionnaire in appendix A).[3] Notably, the largest programmatic cost expenditures for prisons have been for health care and education. And, interestingly, a survey completed by the NIC indicated that health care and educational programs were the most frequently contracted for by a majority of states' facilities (Camp and Camp 1984). This study includes a comparison of health care and educational programs for each facility. Overall cost information was gathered by contacting the appropriate contractor or funding agent and obtaining copies of contracts and budgets.

What follows is a comparison of our findings at the Weaversville Intensive Treatment Unit located in Northampton, Pennsylvania and operated by RCA, with the North Central Secure Treatment Unit located in Danville, Pennsylvania and operated by the Pennsylvania Department of Public Welfare.

The Weaversville Intensive Treatment Unit, previously owned and operated by RCA but purchased by General Electric in 1986, has been in operation as a maximum security juvenile detention center since 1976.[4] The building, once part of a large state-operated dairy farm complex, is a large, two-story, brick, schoolhouse-like structure over twenty-five years old. The structure is surrounded by eight-foot fences, topped with straight and scroll barbed wire. All entranceways and hallway doors are kept locked. Windows are secured with locked screens. Two outdoor recreation areas are also fenced and surrounded by barbed wire. The unit is located in rural Northampton, Pennsylvania, approximately one and one-half hours from Philadelphia. An airport is within two miles and major roadways are nearby.

The condition of the privately-operated Northampton facility is fair. It is in need of paint and minor repairs. Inmate rooms are drab and need improvement. The general impression one receives while at the facility is that it is well-worn. Its rated capacity—that is, the number of inmates the facility is built to house—is twenty-six. The average daily occupancy in 1988 was approximately twenty-six inmates.

The director utilizes a progressive point system to motivate inmates toward better behavior. His leadership style could be considered democratic. Leadership style, whether democratic, authoritarian, or laissez-faire (as described in the classic 1939 study completed by Lewin, Lippit, and White) can impact on program costs in significant ways (Lawler 1973). Differences in leadership styles may account for some of the differences in the operational costs of two facilites. The democratic management style is defined as leadership that encourages group discussion and group decision-making. The basic inmate treatment philosophy is rehabilitative rather than punitive. The administration-to-inmate ratio (administration includes administrators, counselors, cooks, assistants, maintenance staff, and so forth) is twenty-five to twenty-six, or nearly one for one. The teacher-to-inmate ratio is five to twenty-six, or one teacher for just over five inmates.

The health care available to inmates is extensive. RCA utilizes local professionals including physicians, eye doctors, dentists, and hospital staff, on an as-needed basis. Upon assignment to Weaversville, all inmates are given a physical, eye examination, and dental checkup. All health care is paid through RCA's health insurance system, the premiums for which are included as a contracted cost. In case of emergency conditions such as a hepatitis outbreak or measles, the state will pay for medical care under a "miscellaneous encumbrances" clause in the original contract.

Educational classes are provided by, and are the responsibility of, the Northampton School District. RCA oversees the education program and provides remedial training and vocational education in fields such as plumbing, bricklaying, and small engine repair. General Education Diploma (G.E.D.) classes are emphasized. There is no computer or electronics training being given. RCA does not participate in government grant programs such as Title 20 or JETPA, which provide funds for training purposes.

The North Central Secure Treatment Unit, operated and managed by the Pennsylvania State Department of Public Welfare, is a maximum-security juvenile detention center. It is located in rural Pennsylvania, about two miles from the City of Danville and two hours drive from Harrisburg. The area is accessible by major highways. The structure, once part of the Danville Psychiatric Hospital and located behind the hospital complex, is well over twenty-five years old. It is a three-story, schoolhouse-like brick building, completely surrounded by an eight-foot fence, topped with straight and scrolled barbed wire. A voice-activated intercom connects the front and back gates with the interior reception area. Doors and hallways are all locked and windows are screen-locked. The building is approximately a third or more larger than the privately-operated RCA Weaversville facility.[5]

The publicly-operated North Central's rates capacity is twenty-eight beds. On the average, twenty-six of these beds are occupied. The manager exhibits a more authoritarian leadership approach than is the case with the manager of the Weaversville facility (Lawler 1973). There is an emphasis on obedience as well as rehabilitation as the means to increasing inmate self-esteem and personal worth.

The administration-to-inmate ratio is thirty-one to twenty-six, or more than 1.25 administrative staff to each inmate. The teacher-to-inmate ratio is close to one to five.

Health care services in this publicly-owned and operated facility are similar to those provided by the RCA facility. A part-time nurse, however, is on the premises five days a week.

Educational classes at Danville are the responsibility of the Danville School District. Emphasis is placed on General Education Diploma (GED) preparation, but average lengths of stays at the public Danville institution are such that not many inmates can avail themselves of the program. The Danville Unit provides "telecom" courses with local schools that allow a small number of inmates to listen in on ongoing classes at local schools. Ten computer terminals and software packages are available as training aids for inmates, something not provided in the privately operated facility. The Danville Unit takes advantage of four educational grant programs from state and local governments (Title I, Title XX, JETPA, and Corrections Education Grant) to provide specialized computer training to its students. The facility also has a small engine repair shop for use in vocational training.

Utilizing an evaluation form adapted from one developed by George and Camille Camp, the programs and services that are available at each institution were identified and listed in Table 4.1. The private facility just edges out the public facility in number of services being provided.

The Pennsylvania Department of Youth and Family Services monitors costs for all secure and non-secure facilities operated by the State.[6] Table 4.2 provides information collected by the state regarding inmates per diem costs. Table 4.2 reveals that the privately-operated RCA facility has less per diem costs per person than the publicly-operated North Central facility. Of the five juvenile facilities (Weaversville, Southeast, North Central, New Castle, and Bensalem), Weaversville, the only privately-operated facility, is by far less costly to operate than the other four state-operated facilities, according to the state's own analyses.[7]

Table 4.3 shows that the privately-operated RCA prison provides more for its per diem costs than does the publicly-operated facility. Note that not only is the per diem cost per inmate much lower in the private facility but also when weighted by the number of services comparable to the public facility, the per diem cost differential between the two facilities is even greater.

Table 4.4 provides a summary comparison of the privately-operated RCA-Weaversville Intensive Treatment Unit with the publicly-operated North Central Intensive Secure Treatment Unit. The facilities are nearly identical. Weaversville has a better administrator-to-inmate ratio and operates with a more democratic style of management. Also, Weaversville educational programs include more vocational instruction than Danville.

Our second comparison will be between the Butler County Jail located in Butler, Pennsylvania and operated by the Buckingham Security organization, with the Salem County Jail located in Salem, New Jersey and operated by the Salem County government.

At the time this study was performed, the Butler County Jail was operated by Buckingham Security, L.T.D. It is a turn-of-the-century, maximum-security facility, used to detain mostly short-term county inmates as well as overflow state inmates and a few federal felons.[8] The building is an old, square, factory-type structure of two floors and a basement, where prisoners are held in four main blocks with ten cells per block. Each block contains twenty prisoners. Blocks are segregated by class of inmate. Inmates leave cell blocks periodically for outdoor recreation, use of the library, meeting with visitors, meals, et cetera. Inmates are heavily guarded at all times.

Cameras are used extensively to monitor inmate entrances and exists. There are many windows near each block allowing for daylight and a view of the outside.

The facility is located in the heart of Butler, Pennsylvania, a small city located about an hour north of Pittsburgh, and near to an airport and other modes of transportation. The privately-operated County Jail is clean, painted, and well-kept. Overcrowding is not a problem. The rated capacity of the building is 106 beds. The average daily occupancy is ninety-six inmates.

The private manager of the Butler County Jail utilizes a democratic management style to facilitate supervisor, guard, and inmate problem-solving whenever possible. The general penal philosophy is a mix of rehabilitative and punitive. The average length of stay being six months generally dictates that the facility emphasizes detention over rehabilitation. However, attempts are made, given the democratic management style, to assist rehabilitation by allowing religious and other groups on premises to provide services and counselling to the inmates.

The administration to inmate ratio is nine to ninety or one administrative staff to every ten inmates. The guards to inmates ratio is twenty-one to ninety, or about one guard for every four inmates.

Health care available to inmates at the Butler County Jail is comprehensive and includes physicians who are on call, dental care, mental health counseling, eye care, and hospital needs. Educational services include remedial training for completion of the GED program and a growing library of reference and fiction materials. Table 4.5 provides a summary of all the services available to inmates at the privately-operated Butler County and publicly-operated Salem County Jails.

It must be noted here that the Butler County Prison guards were county civil service employees even as the facility was managed by a private company. When the private contract was negotiated, provisions were made for the guards to remain paid by the county, retaining most county benefits, but the supervision and hiring/firing responsibility was delegated to the Buckingham Security Company. In comparing per diem costs with the Salem County Jail, labor costs for guards were not compared, allowing the comparison to be more true.

The Salem County Jail, located in Salem County, New Jersey, is a government-operated maximum security county prison.[9] Very similar to the Butler County Jail, this turn-of-the-century, three-floor building is secured to such a degree that windows cannot be opened to let in air or provide inmates with an outside view. There are no security cameras. All surveillance is performed by security officers making rounds. No recreation area exists. In fact, overcrowding forced the gymnasium to be turned into a cell block. Prisoners do not go outside, nor have any inside exercise, unless they are lucky enough to be one of approximately ten inmates who are on work-release.

The jail is located in the center of Salem, New Jersey, a small city approximately one hour's drive from Philadelphia, with access to a major airport and water routes, as well as major highways and other forms of transportation.

The condition of the publicly-operated jail is poor by any standards. It is unkempt, in need of paint and repair, and houses inmates in open bay blocks with virtually no privacy or place for relaxation. Without access to outside recreation or inside recreation, or even windows to view the outside and let in light, the internal conditions are not unlike what one might perceive the conditions to have been in a medieval dungeon except for a color TV that hangs perversely from the wall of each crowded cell block.

The rated capacity of the Salem County facility is 95 inmates. Current average occupancy, however, is 185. Much of the overcrowding is due to state prisoners not being transferred to state facilities. The underwarden's leadership style is laissez-faire (Lawler 1973). Mostly, however, he practices benign neglect with respect to the needs of the prisoners as a result of the county government's refusal to increase space or money for the care of the prisoners. The penal philosophy pervasive here is punitive, with no attempt at rehabilitation.

The administration to inmate ratio is 8 to 184, or 1 administrative staff to 23 inmates. The guard to inmate ratio is 40 to 184, or 1 guard to every 4.6 inmates. These figures, when compared to the privately-operated Butler County Jail, show a significantly worse staff ratio. Combining this information with the tremendous difference between the two facilities' conditions and available services is meaningful when analyzing the cost-per-inmate figures in table 4.6.

The health care services are comprehensive but include no mental health care. A full-time nurse is on duty five days a week. The education programs available are minimal and include only GED materials. Not many inmates take advantage of the limited educational opportunity, given the tight quarters and lack of study space. The Salem County facility has a videocassette system where movies can be played through the system of televisions in the cell blocks.

Table 4.6 is an analysis of costs per inmate. Table 4.7 is a summary comparison of the privately-operated Butler County Jail with the publicly-operated Salem County Jail.

The final comparison is between the Silverdale Detention Center located at Chattanooga, Tennessee and operated by the Correction Corporation of America, and the Warren County Correctional Center located at Belvidere, New Jersey, and operated by the Warren County government.

The Silverdale Detention Center has been operated by the Corrections Corporation of America (CCA) since October 1984.[10] This facility, known as the Hamilton County Work Farm until its takeover by CCA had been operated by the Hamilton County government since the 1930s. Since CCA's receipt of a contract to operate this facility, it has built several new buildings, including cell blocks, a library, offices, and a new dining hall. The two main cell blocks are modern facilities with two floors each, extensive visual capability, cameras, and automatic locking systems. Cell blocks have central control stations manned by guards with access to sophisticated radio, telephone, walkie-talkie, and TV monitoring devices. A separate women's facility exists in an older, smaller building.

The prison grounds are located in a semi-rural area, approximately one-half hour's drive from Chattanooga, with access to air, rail, and bus transport, as well as being situated near major roadways.

The general condition of the CCA structures and grounds are clean, new, and well maintained. The cell blocks have individual cells and include color televisions and pool tables in group areas.

Table 4.1
Services That Exist At Or Are Available To Each Facility

	RCA (Private)	NC (Public)
Transportation	x	x
Vocational Programs	x	x
Educational Programs	x	x
Video Programming		
Religious Programming	x	x
After Care	x	
Drug Treatment	x	x
Mental Health Programs	x	x
Health Services	x	x
Inhouse Inmate Labor	x	x
College Program	x	
Cultural Program		
Inmate Businesses		
Work Release	x	
Staff Training	x	x
Office Computers	x	x
Inmate Computers	x	x
Drama, Dancing, etc.	x	x
Canteen, Commissary		x

Physicians, Nutritionists	x	x
Hobby and Crafts		
Recreational Therapy	x	x
Sex Offender Therapy	x	x
Laundry Service		x
Maintenance	x	x
Counselling	x	x
	20	19

Source: Information collected during on-site interviews. This listing is adapted from the NIJ study performed by George and Camille Camp, *Private Sector Involvement in Prison Services and Operation*, NIJ, U.S. Department of Justice (February 1984), appendix.

Table 4.2
Costs Per Day Per Inmate (Department of Welfare)

	RCA (Private)	North Central (Public)
1 July, 1985	$130	$141
1 July, 1986	119	123
1 Jan., 1987	105	123
3 year average:	$118	$129
Weighted 3 year average*	$118	$136

Source: Pennsylvania State Department of Public Welfare, *Children, Youth and Families Bulletin*, Harrisburg, Pennsylvania; Department of Public Welfare, 1985, 1986 and 1987.

* Weighted three-year average figures were calculated by dividing the three-year average cost figure by the number of services available, then multiplying the "cost-per-service" figure for each facility by the number of services available at the facility with the largest number of services. This allows a truer comparison of costs if both facilities had an equal number of programs/services available.

Table 4.3
Costs Per Inmate (This Study)

	RCA (Private)	North Central (Public)
FY 85	$872,752	$1,265,916
FY 86	845,009	1,270,734
FY 87	872,115	—

Average	$863,292	$1,268,325
Average Number of Inmates	26	26
Annual Per Diem	$33,203	$48,781
Per Diem	$91.00	$134.00
Weighted 3 year average*	$91.00	$141.00

Sources: Figures for the Public North Central's expenditures were collected from telephone conversations with and information received from Dale Ankelrandt of the Pennsylvania Division of Children, Youth and Families.

Figures for the private RCA-Weaversville expenditures were collected from telephone discussions with and information received from Jack Godlesky of Pennsylvania's Division of Children, Youth and Families.

* Weighted 3 year average figures were calculated by dividing the 3 year average cost figure by the number of services available, then multiplying the "cost-per-service" figure for each facility by the number of services available at the facility with the largest number of services. This allows a truer comparison of costs if both facilities had an equal number of programs/services available.

Table 4.4
Summary Comparison of Weaversville and North Central

	Weaversville (Private)	North Central (Public)
Structure:	Max. Secure, old, 2 flrs.	Max. Secure, old. 3 flrs.
Location:	Rural, transport avail.	Rural, transport avail.
Condition:	Fair, worn	Freshly painted, clean
Capacity:	26 beds	28 beds
Occupancy:	26 inmates	26 inmates
Management style:	Democratic	Authoritarian
Penal philosophy:	Rehabilitative	Rehabilitative
Admin/Inmate ratio:	1:1	1.25:1
Teacher/Inmate ratio:	1:5	1:5
Health care:	Comprehensive	Comprehensive, plus nurse on duty
Educ. programs:	More vocational	computers, govt grants
Total services:	20	19
State per diem:*	$118.00	$136.00

Study per diem:	$ 91.00	$134.00
Weighted per diem:	$ 91.00	$141.00

Source: Data collected during and as a result of on-site visits to the private RCA-Weaversville Intensive Treatment Unit, 3 September, 1987 and the public North Central Intensive Treatment Unit, 28 September, 1987.

* Figures provided by Pennsylvania Department of Welfare, *Children, Youth and Families Bulletins* (1985, 1986, 1987).

Table 4.5
Services That Exist At Or Are Available To Each Facility

	Butler Co. Jail (Private)	Salem Co. Jail (Private)
Transportation	x	x
Vocational Programs		
Educational Programs	x	x
Video Programming		x
Religious Programming	x	x
After Care		
Drug Treatment	x	
Mental Health Programs	x	
Health Services	x	x
Inhouse Inmate Labor	x	x
College Program	x	x
Cultural Program		
Inmate Businesses		
Work Release	x	x
Staff Training	x	x
Office Computers	x	
Inmate Computers		
Drama, Dancing, etc.		
Canteen, Commissary	x	x
Physicians, Nutritionists	x	x
Hobby and Crafts		
Recreational Therapy	x	
Sex Offender Therapy	x	x
Laundry Service	x	x
Maintenance	x	x
Counselling	x	—
	18	14

Source: Information collected during on-site interviews. This listing is adapted from the NIJ study performed by George and Camille Camp, *Private Sector Involvement in Prison Services and Operation*, NIJ, U.S. Department of Justice (February 1984), appendix.

Table 4.6
Costs Per Inmate

	Butler County (Private)	Salem County (Public)
FY 87	$999,422	$1,320,218
Average Number of Inmates	96 (not including state inmates)	144 (not including state inmates)
Annual Per Diem:	$10,410	$9,168
Per Diem:	$28.52	$25.11*
Weighted average**	$28.52	$32.29

Sources: Figures for private Butler County Prison's expenditures were collected from telephone conversations with and information received from Tom Labvorini, Butler County Treasurer.

Figures for public Salem County Prison's expenditures were collected from telephone conversations with and information received from Lee Munyon, Treasurer's Office, Salem County, New Jersey.

* The tremendous overcrowding problem experienced by Salem County Jail tends to unfairly decrease the prisoner per diem costs. When weighted for available services and programs, Salem County's per diem increases significantly.

** Weighted three-year average figures were calculated by dividing the three-year average cost figure by the number of services available, then multiplying the "cost-per-service" figure for each facility by the number of services available at the facility with the largest number of services. This allows a truer comparison of costs if both facilities had an equal number of programs/services available.

Table 4.7
Summary Comparison of Butler County Jail and Salem County Jail

	Butler County (Private)	Salem County (Public)
Structure:	Max. Secure, old, 3 flrs.	Max. Secure, old., 2 flrs.
Location:	Urban, center city	Urban, center city
Condition:	Good, well kept	Bad, poorly kept
Capacity:	106 beds	95 beds
Occupancy:	96 inmates	184 inmates
Management style:	Democratic	Laissez-faire
Penal philosophy:	Rehabilitative-Punitive	Punitive
Admin/Inmate ratio:	1:10	1:23

Guard/Inmate ratio:	1:4.2	1:46
Health care:	Comprehensive	Comprehensive, no mental health
Educ. programs:	GED, library	GED, videos
Total services:	18	14
Inmate per diem:	$28.52	$25.11
Weighted per diem:	$28.52	$32.29

Source: Data was collected during and subsequent to on-site visits to Butler County Jail, 8 September, 1987 and Salem County Jail, 5 October, 1987.

The prevailing management style is democratic-participative. The prison manager attempts to include inmates in all phases of decision-making and, by agreement, must include county government input when developing operational alternatives or finalizing management decisions. The basic penal philosophy used is one of rehabilitation.

The administration to inmate ratio is 20 administrative staff to 375 inmates, or one staff for every 19 inmates. The guard to inmate ratio is 60 guards to 375 inmates, or one guard for every 6.25 inmates.

Health care at this privately-managed facility is comprehensive. The facility has three full-time nurses. All health care is provided as needed and contracted for in advance by CCA. Educational services include testing center for remedial training. Literacy programs are emphasized. Religious education is available, as is a reference and fiction library. Inmates can attend vocational or college courses if approved by the courts and if the inmate had been attending courses prior to his or her conviction.

The Warren County Correctional Center, located in Warren County, New Jersey, is a new public facility, in operation since August 1986.[11] All buildings consist of separate two-story cell blocks for inmates, each with individual cells, televisions, and group tables. Buildings are connected by enclosed corridors. Each cell block is monitored by a guard utilizing the newest technology including computerized monitoring for fire, water pressure changes, smoke, gas leaks, and prisoner location. Microwave prisoner-escape detection systems are also used. All doors open electronically and are monitored by voice and camera. Library and recreation facilities are large well-equipped.

The public facility is located in rural Warren County, New Jersey, fifteen minutes from the City of Belvidere and about a two-hour drive from Philadelphia and a one-hour drive from New York City. There is access to major roadways.

The condition of the public facility is very good, clean, and modern. The rated capacity is 87 inmates, current occupancy is 109 inmates. This facility is already overcrowded.

The management style utilized in the Warren County facility is democratic-participative. Access to the warden and staff members is emphasized and encouraged by the administration. Ideas are solicited from inmates and guards for a collective problem-solving council. The general penal philosophy that prevails is punitive-rehabilitative. However, management finds that convicts spend much of their time trying to find legal ways to get out rather than being rehabilitated.

The administrative staff to inmate ratio is 6 to 109, or one administrative staff person to every 18 inmates. The guard to inmate ratio is 55 to 109, or one guard to every two inmates.

Health care at the public Warren Correctional Center is comprehensive and includes twenty-four-hour on-call nursing with four full-time nurses. Educational services are similar to those provided at the privately-operated Silverdale facility. Vocational and college leave is possible, and the library has good resources.

Table 4.8 indicates that there are fewer programs and services available at the publicly-operated Warren Center than at the privately-operated Silverdale Center. Table 4.9 shows that the Silverdale facility is much less expensive to operate than the Warren County facility. Table 4.10 is a summary comparison of costs and programs for both institutions.

Table 4.11 summarizes the inmate per diem rates of all six institutions. As can be seen by the table, all three privately-operated facilities operate at less cost than the three publicly-operated facilities. The greatest cost differential is between Weaversville (private) and Danville (public). Observations mentioned earlier implied that RCA is not putting a lot of money into upkeep or in special training such as the use of computers. Also, Danville has a more sophisticated physical education program. The smallest cost differential is between the Butler County Prison and the Salem County Jail. As noted, the Butler County Prison is not overcrowded. However, the Salem County Jail is holding nearly twice the number of inmates than it is rated to house. This may be a cause for the Salem County Jail per diem rate being as low as it is.

Barriers to Entry-Overcome by Private Contractors

This study has identified over fifty issues that, according to the available literature and discussions with prison officials and officials within the criminal justice system, have surfaced as points of contention between proponents and opponents of prison privatization.[12] These issues were earlier separated into five categories: political, administrative, financial, legal, and social issues. The more significant of these issues have been examined in more detail as "barriers to entry" to the private prison market. It is important to determine how various "barriers" that seem to be more controversial and far reaching than the rest have been overcome by the three private prison operators who are a part of this study.

The first of these issues is the political issue of whether democracy is circumvented by contracting out the operation of a prison. All three private prison operators thought this issue to be meaningless. They argued that government circumvents "democracy" any time that representatives believe their actions to be in "the best interests" of society. The Weaversville operator said that government practices "eminent domain" and "zoning waivers" that circumvent the democratic process.

Table 4.8
Services That Exist At Or Are Available To Each Facility

	Silverdale (Private)	Warren County (Public)
Transportation	x	x
Vocational Programs		
Educational Programs	x	x
Video Programming	x	
Religious Programming	x	x
After Care	x	
Drug Treatment	x	x
Mental Health Programs	x	x
Health Services	x	x
Inhouse Inmate Labor	x	x
Off premises inmate labor	x	
College Program		
Cultural Program		x
Inmate Businesses		
Work Release	x	x
Staff Training	x	x
Office Computers	x	x
Inmate Computers		
Drama, Dancing, etc.		x
Canteen, Commissary	x	
Physicians, Nutritionists	x	x
Hobby and Crafts		
Recreational Therapy	x	x

Sex Offender Therapy
Laundry Service	x	x
Counselling	x	x
Total	18	16

Source: Information collected during on-site interviews. This listing is adapted from the NIJ study performed by George and Camille Camp, *Private Sector Involvement in Prison Services and Operation*, NIJ, U.S. Department of Justice (February 1984), appendix.

Table 4.9
Costs Per Inmate

	Silverdale (Private)	Warren County (Public)
FY 86	$2,357,082	$1,523,118
FY 87	$2,897,595	$1,894,206
2 year average	$2,627,338	$1,708,662
Average number of inmates	375	109
Annual per inmate	$7,006	$15,675
Per diem	$19.00	$43.00
Weighted 3 year average*	$19.00	$48.00

Sources: Figures for expenditures for the private Silverdale Detention Center were collected from telephone discussion with and information received from Kathy Walker of the Hamilton County, Tennessee, Administration.

Figures for expenditures for the public Warren County Correctional Center were collected from telephone discussion and information received from Daniel Olshefsi, Senior Accountant with the county treasurer of Warren County.

* Weighted two-year average figures were calculated by dividing the two-year average cost figure by the number of services available, then multiplying the "cost-per-service" figure for each facility by the number of services available at the facility with the largest number of services. This allows a truer comparison of costs if both facilities had an equal number of programs/services available.

Table 4.10
Summary Comparison of the Silverdale Detention and Warren County correctional Centers

	Silverdale (Private)	Warren County (Public)
Structure:	Max. Secure, new, electronic	Max. Secure, new, electronic

Location:	Semi-rural, near large city	Rural
Condition:	New, clean, modern	New, clean, modern
Capacity:	350 beds	87 beds
Occupancy:	375 inmates	109 inmates
Management style:	Democratic-partic.	Democratic-partic.
Penal philosophy:	Rehab.-Punitive	Rehab.-Punitive
Admin/Inmate ratio:	1:19	1.19
Guard/Inmate ratio:	1:6.25	1:2
Health care:	Comprehensive, 3 nurses and mental health	Comprehensive, 4 nurses
Educ. programs:	GED, literacy, remed, Vocat., college	GED, Vocat., college
Total services:	18	16
Inmate per diem:	$19.00	$43.00
Weighted per diem:	$19.00	$48.00

Source: Data was collected during and subsequent to on-site visits to Silverdale Detention Center, 14 and 15 September and Warren county Correctional Center, 6 October, 1987.

Table 4.11
Summary of Weighted Daily Prison Costs Per Inmate

Private	Per Diem	Public	Per Diem
Weaversville	$91.00	North Central	$141.00
Butler	$28.52	Salem	$32.29
Silverdale	$19.00	Warren	$48.00
Average Per Diem (Private)	$46.17	Average Per Diem (Public)	$73.76

Source: Compiled by the author from the information received during interviews, during telephone conversations, from written correspondence and from copies of budgets and cost statements from the six prisons visited.

A second important issue is the administrative argument that private operators hire fewer and less qualified personnel (guards, nurses, administrative staff, cooks) in order to reap profits and that this practice impacts directly on the level and quality of treatment afforded to prisoners. Each private operator addressed this issue differently. The Weaversville operator responded that RCA has an image to uphold and could not risk treating prisoners poorly given its other business involvement. Weaversville also said that providing more and better services is a way of getting a larger contract. Weaversville stated that the training, hiring criteria, and types and number of administrative components such as nurses, cooks, and counselors are stated explicitly in the contract. The real difference the respondents argued between public and private personnel-hiring practices is that private operators are not constrained by civil service requirements and therefore employees must fulfill their job duties or be replaced. The Silverdale private manager agreed with the Weaversville operator and pointed out that their facility never had a chaplain, library, or as many programs and services as it now does. The Butler private manager argued that they stay attuned to the American Correctional Association (ACA) guidelines on personnel training and facility environment to ensure good treatment and service to inmates. Finally, the private operators believe that unions, such as AFGE and AFSCME, have inflated this issue fearing a loss to union membership and union dues.

A second administrative issue revolves around the absence of standards or guidelines for the operation of a private prison and for the training of prison personnel, especially guards. Both private county operators indicated that strict state standards exist that they must adhere to. The Butler County Jail operator pointed out that they follow the ACA guidelines for operating the prison and ensuring that guards are properly trained. The Weaversville Juvenile Center operator indicated that they adhere to the Pennsylvania Department of Welfare Guidelines and are monitored for compliance, semi-annually. Moreover, the Weaversville operator responded that the RCA-Pennsylvania contract sets down in detail staff experience and training requirements. A discussion of this issue with staff of the New Jersey Department of Corrections established that nearly all states have a manual of standards and guidance for counties on the operation of jails and prisons. Notably, the New Jersey Manual of Standards has an entire section dedicated to staff training and guidance and several sections outlining jail operations (New Jersey...1979). For instance, the Section titled "Reception Orientation, Release and Property Control" sets forth procedures to be used when a new inmate arrives, including gathering personal information, storage of personal belongings, and arranging for a cell.

One of the financial issues presented earlier is the barrier to private entry into prison management occasioned by high liability costs. Discussions with private prison operators revealed that liability can be claimed against both the state and the private company, which could reduce the state's direct liability claim totals while at the same time shifting some of the private operator's liability claims back to the state through contract costs. However, all private operators agreed that they are extremely attentive to the possibility of liability claims and implement preventive measures more often than public operators because high claims impact directly on net profits through higher insurance costs. The Weaversville and Silverdale private operators were able to overcome initial high insurance premium costs because these costs are integrated into parent companies' insurance packages. The private Butler operator claims that the high cost of liability insurance will be reduced with time as their record becomes recognized. Efficient operation, they argue, allows them enough revenue to pay the high permiums.

One legal issue discussed with prison managers was the delegation of prison operations to a private company and its constitutionality. All three private operators agree that the delegation of the managerial and operational functions by a government body through legal contract to a private entrepreneur is constitutional. Some states such as Tennessee, where Silverdale is located, have enabling legislation that supports this view (Dunham 1986).

A second legal/constitutional issue is whether police power, or the use of deadly force, should be delegated to staff members of private companies. None of the private or public facilities visited maintain armed guards inside their facilities. The county facilities, public and private, all maintained ammunition and armor cabinets, and ensured that all of the guards were trained in use of weapons and riot control. The guard force at privately-operated Butler Prison continues to be made up of civil service county employees who see no significant difference in their duties now as compared with the duties they had before the private company began managing the facility. The guard force at Silverdale also consists of mostly the same employees that were in place when it was publicly operated. Interviews with these guards revealed that they sae no significant difference in their duties. There was some concern by the guards that as they were no longer deputized, inmate-guard provocations could increase. However, according to the facility administrator, provocations between the guards and the inmate population have not increased. Loss of deputization is more a loss of personal status than a loss of authority over inmates. It should be noted that deadly force had not been used at any of the private facilities visited during the tenure of the private operators. Escapes and personal confrontations do occur but are reacted to or resolved by the same methods traditionally used:

physically overpowering inmates, depriving inmates of prison privileges, and depriving inmates of "good time."

The last legal/constitutional issue has to do with the denial of parole, the loss of "good time," and the application of discipline. Abuses would permit the private prison operator increased profits by extending the stay of prisoners in their institutions. All three private facilities maintain government-approved procedures for decreasing good time, invoking disciplinary sanctions, and paroling convicts. Parole is basically a state function. County courts grant good time at the beginning of a sentence and assume the inmate will be released early unless good time is decreased. Reduction of good time occurs as a sanction (in both public and private facilities) only after all other types of sanctions have been invoked such as loss of privileges, loss of visitation rights, or detention in the cell. Moreover, all three private operators interviewed do utilize a third party in the disciplinary process. At Silverdale, a county employee, the Classification Officer, participates in all disciplinary decision-making hearings and has the authority to strike down or modify the hearing recommendations. The hearings performed at the Butler facility are attended by prison guard officers who also happen to be county employees. The Weaversville operator explained that there are so many outsiders (such as lawyers, family members, probation and parole officials, the courts, and the press) watching disciplinary proceedings that no private company could supplant the proper criminal justice decision-making process to further its own profit goals without notice. However, this is one issue area that would need careful monitoring should prison privatization expand in this country. The profit motive, while making for greater efficiency in prison management could, in some cases, be subversive of prisoner rights.

Public Operators' Views On Barriers and Costs

Structured interviews with officials of public correctional facilities, as explained in detail earlier in this chapter, showed that a marked difference exists between what the public officials believe to be the most significant problems with privatization of prisons, and what problems the private officials themselves recognize. Utilizing the questionnaire in appendix A, it was found that every public operator believes that liability insurance costs are too high for private operators to pay. As indicated earlier, RCA and CCA both shift these costs into the parent companies' insurance structures. It must be recognized, however, that parent companies cannot absorb these costs for too long. Moreover, liability costs may preclude small independent companies from competing for prison management contracts. Notably, private operators claim to be more conscious of insurance liability claims than public operators and maintain a preventative defense against them. At the time of the on-site visits, each private operator claimed to not have had any significant claims pressed against them.

Public operators cited personnel problems and turnover as a significant problem for private operators due to lower salaries and the lack of government benefits and perquisites. However, all three private operators' salary structures are the same or higher than comparative government salaries and benefits, and perquisites have not decreased. Public operators argue that salaries in private industry remain the same only if non-salary benefits decline and/or the number of staff decreases. This study showed, however, that staff-to-inmate ratios favor the privately-operated facilities. It should be noted too that the private operators' claim of the ability to use employees efficiently coupled with the fact that employees can more quickly be fired, may be the reason why private facilities can operate with less employee costs. Some private employees are happier with company stock options and company health benefits than with the county benefits and retirement plan and some are not as happy. RCA employees do have good educational benefits. Different areas within RCA and General Electric are now viewed as possible career paths, whereas youth counseling with the state was viewed as having its limits for promotion.

Public operators maintained that inmate medical costs would prove to be prohibitive for private vendors. One can observe from this chapter's comparative analyses (Tables 4.4, 4.7, and 4.10) that health care at the private facilities is equal to (and in one instance better than) health care available at public facilities.

Another issue suggested by the public operators as a significant stumbling block to private operators is the ability to meet minimum state standards on low budget. All of the private operations at the time of the study had approved contracts and had undergone program and fiscal audits, and none were operating with major audit exceptions.

An issue raised by the public operators as a problem with private operations is that private operators should not be authorized to use deadly force with inmates. None of the private operators interviewed has ever had the occasion to use deadly force. The strength of this issue will have to wait to be tested.

Private Operators' Views on Barriers and Costs

During the on-site visits, private operators articulated what they believed to be the real barriers to entering the private prison market and to operating a privately-managed prison. Two main themes arose during interviews: politics and unions. All three private operators argued that state and county employee unions are inflating all the issues dramatically for fear of losing union membership and dues revenues. There was also the view that unions and other lobby groups wield too much power and are smothering the private prison movement. This perception is arguable given that prison guards are only a relatively small percentage of the entire population of federal, state, and local civil servants. Also, the power the union or prison interest groups wield, though significant, is probably no more than the political power wielded by business interest groups.

The Butler and Silverdale operators, both of whom contract with county governments, indicated a sensitivity to the balance of power within their respective boards of county commissioners as commissioners' views on private prison operations and contract decisions impact operations directly.

The Butler operator said that even after three years of contracting with the county, there is only a slim majority of commissioners who continue to support the company, even though the overall cost of the jail has decreased. The main problem causing the lack of political support, they said, is the misconception common among criminal justice and political officials regarding the costs, constitutionality, and political benefit of contracting out for prison management.

Notably, administrative staff members mentioned that even after years of operation, local politicians and community officials continue to have reservations about having the local jail "run by corporate executives", even though the Silverdale warden is a seventeen-year veteran of the Texas corrections system and the Butler County Jail operator has twenty years of corrections experience.

The other obstacles to market entry mentioned by private operators include a lack of capital and high insurance costs, the latter of which was discussed earlier.

As noted earlier, inmate per diem cost of operating the three private prisons was less than the cost of operating the three public prisons. For instance, the private Weaversville weighted per diem cost is $91.00 per inmate, where the public North Central cost is $141.00 per inmate. The private Butler County Jail weighted per diem cost is $28.52 per inmate, where the public Salem County Jail cost is $32.39. The private Silverdale Center cost is $19.00 per inmate, where the public Warren County Jail is $48.00.

Why are the three privately-operated prison facilities significantly less costly to operate than the three similar public prison facilities included in this study? There are some responses to this question that were common to all three private prison management teams, and some particular to each. The first cost-saving measure is the way private operators purchase food, clothing, and services. There is no long, complicated bidding process. Private prison managers can buy locally-produced products in bulk and take advantage of discounts when they become available. Private operators do not have to take the lowest bid, which means they can purchase better quality items that last longer. The private operators claim they have less waste. Food portions are now better accounted for. In one instance, Butler County prison, when it was still publicly operated, was purchasing too much meat for inmates. Now, as a privately-owned facility, the prison is using a nutritionally-balanced meal plan and saving money. The private operations have better accounting methods and processes. All three private prisons are using personal computers to store and sort information. Also, the private operators are audited not only by the contractor but by the parent company as well.

Private operators are close to the inmates needs. The Warden-Manager knows the budget, keeps an eye on saving, is responsible for purchasing and hiring, and can run the prison utilizing business management principles, unfettered by public bureaucracy and public officials making important decisions from afar.

As explained by private prison operators, the staff is more flexibly hired and more efficiently utilized. Staff can be hired temporarily if necessary, instead of using overtime. In private facilities, raises are given by merit, as compared to many public institutions where raises are automatic. Unproductive employees can be let go when necessary. Also, the private-prison operators were having inmates do work, where possible. Inmates earned money in-house, part of which was being returned to the facility in partial payment for their keep. For example, the manager of the private Butler County Jail had many inmates working at prison jobs including meal preparation, cleaning, and library monitoring. The publicly-operated Salem County Jail had no inmates at work within the facility.

Lastly, and very significant, privately-operated Silverdale was able to build two new buildings in five months, a feat not manageable by too many public agencies.

In summary, the three privately-operated correctional centers proved to be more cost-efficiently operated than their publicly operated counterparts. The reasons for their ability to be more cost-efficient are just those characteristics that cause public enterprise to differ from private enterprise: better control over resources, flexible manpower usage, economies, control over expenditures, and less bureaucracy and union problems. In the next chapter, a discussion about policy-making and private prisons is presented as well as a further look at prison managers' views on a variety of other issues.

5

Prison Privatization and Public Policy

Policy-making Process

The process of making public policy involves many actors including all of the institutions of government and a variety of entities from outside of the governmental system. A policy is a course of action, a direction taken by government and followed by lawmakers and public officials who are in ideological agreement with the policy and who agree to its direction. They may follow policy or implement policy because of loyalty to the administration or because they lack opposition information that would otherwise cause them to move in some independent direction.

Policy-making is a process of developing laws, policies, procedures, and even perceptions and points of view that evolve over time from the ongoing information synthesizing process of issue networks interested in particular issue areas (Heclo 1978). The issue network that exists that processes information and perceptions about private prisons includes agents such as: INS, AFSCME, ACA, ACLU, PBA, ABA, AFGE, state agencies, media, private vendors, senate and house of Congress and of each state, subcommittees, DOJ, and others including researchers and academics. From all of the discourse, investigating, and searching usually comes movement on an issue. However, in the case of private prisons there has been a noticeable lack of movement.

James Anderson, Thomas Dye, and others have developed models for our use in analyzing public policy-making (Dye 1987; Anderson 1984). The institutional model looks closely at institutions of government such as the judiciary, legislatures, presidency (governorship), and bureaucracy and how they interact or individually impact on the policy-making process. The process model views politics more as a process that is unfolding over time. Using this model, an analyst would review voting behavior, interest-group pressures upon individual political actors, and other process phenomenon. The group model (pluralist model) presumes that policy-making is significantly affected by the many interests in American society, and therefore studying interest and pressure groups can improve our understanding of how policy is molded and changed to be more pervasively satisfying. The elite model presumes that a powerful elite exists that influences policy-making more than other actors in the system. Here, the analyst attempts to understand these actors and their roles in the process. The rational model is founded upon what Dwight Waldo would call "rational action" (Waldo 1953). One would use this model to attempt to understand policy by determining why and how alternative choices are made, assuming that goals are being pursued in line with the economic principle of maximum social gain and the organizational premise of comprehensive decision-making.

The incremental model analyzes policy upon the premise that most policy is made based on tradition and past experience, with limited time and resources, because man is limited and so are his abilities—referred to as "bounded rationality" by Herbert Simon (Simon 1957).

The game theory model gets its notoriety from the military use of game warfare where opponents attempt to outguess one another using role-playing, simulation, and other techniques. The political systems model allows an analyst to study policy from the point of view that policy is a result of forces in society that come together to form it: actors, environment, other policy, demands and supports, feedback, tradition, and more.

The two models that seem to be most useful in analyzing opponents and supporters of privatization of prisons are the rational model and the Political Systems Model. More often than not, advocates of private prisons are in the private sector and are using the rational model to support their claims of lower costs, efficiency, responsiveness, and the alike. Public officials in corrections and other opposing groups seem more often to be basing their claims of profiteering, risk, and the justice-in-the-public's-hand ideal upon the political systems model. This is as one would expect given the different political and economic orientations of each group. However, it becomes increasingly important in a world of budgetary woes, expanding government deficits, and states with revenue deficiencies, that we are guided by facts and empirical evidence rather than ideology, which tends to alter in direction, stability, and strength over time. This is why it is so important for governments to make available grants to researchers to carry out comparison studies of private and public prisons so that judgments can be made not only by government officials who already have power but, just as importantly, by private industry managers wanting to enter into or develop the private prison market.

Another reason why opponents and supporters of prison

privatization seem to be so far apart in their views comes about through a review of Daniel Elazar's political culture model for analyzing why people vary in the way they believe government should respond to the public (Elazar 1966). Although Elazar's model analyzes a variety of political views corresponding to regional cultures, one could also conclude that opponents and supporters have very different economic and political values. Privateers see the concrete dollars-and-cents issue as dominant, while public leaders see the public-welfare issue as dominant. The question is, "Are both groups' dominant values equally important? Are they reconcilable?" There are many examples of supporters and opponents of programs moving closer together by pilot testing programs or testing innovations over time and on a limited basis to determine the effectiveness and efficiency of new ideas. Some examples are the growth of public medicine in Europe, HMO's in the United States, contracting for mental health services, and contracting for the whole array of social services that at one time government believed could and should only be provided by government. Years ago it was argued that private entrepreneurs should never be allowed to capture the mental health market because the motivation for profit would outweigh patient care. There have been abuses but the private sector has proven itself capable in the social services arena.

Policy Formulation and Adoption

To inspire the public sector to allow private agents access requires that the policy formulation and adoption process be understood by private market managers. Forming policy, according to James Anderson, has three main elements: defining the problem, getting the problem on the agenda, and creating a workable policy (Anderson, 1984). The problem that privatization of prisons is attempting to resolve has been well-defined. Forty-one states and territories are under court order to increase prison floor space and correct other conditions. Bureaucratic "red tape" binds the hands of public officials, even those who have access to funds or alternatives, limiting governmental response to the growing practice of turning convicts out onto the streets because there is nowhere to house them. The problem also includes conflicts in public perceptions of the basic differences between private and public sector corrections. The first operates from a "bottom-line" position. The latter from a "regulatory" position.

Limiting the development of private prison policy is the fact that the issue has not moved from the systemic agenda to the government agenda. Systemically, theorists, government leaders, and citizens are aware of the privatization movement but two things are missing that restrict the issue's movement to the government agenda (the policy-making stage). One is credibility; the other, a triggering mechanism (Waste 1989). An issue will move from the systemic agenda (being discussed and analyzed usually in the academic setting) to the government agenda (where leaders are compelled to look closely at the issue, to create pilot projects, and to provide research grants) when a triggering mechanism, for example an avalanche, explosion, or riot, presses officials into action. The private prison triggering mechanism is currently near firing. We have an avalanche of prisoners sleeping three and four to a cell, or crammed into converted dining halls or gymnasiums. We have an explosion of convicted offenders resulting from the war on drugs, increasing white collar crime, regulatory federalism, and changing morality and ethics. The court system is nearly in a riotous condition, overworked and overwhelmed. Students interning in the courts or with district attorneys offices return to class and talk of increasing numbers of offenders (for higher and higher levels of crime) getting off because the district attorney and the judge realize there is no place to house them, and state law often precludes other alternatives. Students tell of piles of cases never going to trial because the district attorney can't afford to locate the alleged criminals. We become aware of low morale and the disintegration of faith in the system by line officers over judges letting repeat offenders off, time and again.

What is necessary in our policy-making process for a triggering mechanism to have an affect is credibility. Prison privatization has not gained credibility, because there are too few research efforts or comparison studies providing the public and the government with solid, factual, empirical information.

If in the future the prison privatization movement gains momentum and credibility, then policy adoption might take place through one or more of the following mechanisms: bargaining, persuasion, or command (Anderson 1984). State or local politicians might use logrolling techniques or pork-barrel tactics to win state funds for contracting with a private company. Bargains might be struck with public employee unions to ensure the union members are the first to be hired by private companies. Private prison officials would begin lobbying. Interest-group influence would develop. Shareholders would make their preferences known to lawmakers. A governor might take the lead in opening up a major prison to privatization, or legislators might make use of privatization as a useful policy alternative.

Politics of Private of Prisons

Carl Van Horn developed an interesting way to view the politics behind the policy-making process. He uses the terms *boardroom politics, cloakroom politics, chief executive politics, court room politics, living room politics* and *bureaucratic politics* to describe how various groups and actors influence policy-making (Van Horn et al. 1989). For our purposes, a discussion on bureaucratic, cloakroom, chief executive, and living room politics is appropriate. These viewpoints effect the credibility of the prison privatization movement.

Bureaucracy is effected by budgets, the media, regulations, administrative discretion, clientele groups, and other elements. Leaders can influence bureaucracy, but rarely "lead" it, mostly because bureaucracy has a stated mission and specified goals—goals that have existed long before the appointees or newly elected officials showed up, and a mission it does not want to see changed. Bureaucracy seeks to continue the status quo.

Bureaucracy is full of politics. Public officials work in a goldfish bowl, always under the eye of the press, clientele groups, agencies, politicos, and others. It is nearly impossible not to be influenced from outside in this kind of environment. An amorphous public does not have the same influence over privatization decisions as do powerful and cohesive interests. Moreover, the bureaucracy itself is involved in policy-making sometimes more than lawmakers themselves. Bureaucrats lend expertise to developing bills and laws, to molding adopted laws and developing and fine-tuning regulations and procedures. Most state legislatures, when pressed to study the validity of private prisons, have relied on the executive branch corrections departments for studies and statistics. Research completed by a public agency, especially one committed to a particular perception of corrections, may not be the best generator of objective research.

Cloakroom politics, according to Van Horn, is the practice of influencing policy-making from behind closed doors, outside of the public purview and away from public scrutiny. A lot of decisions are either made or tailored in a mayor's office before the staff meeting, in council chambers, in the oval office, or even in the foyer of a restaurant. Our democratic system values public participation and access to the decision process, but our system includes less accessible avenues of policy influence as well. If the ACA can find an opportunity to get the ear of the INS, they will do so and plead their case. If labor representatives can enhance their position by talking with administrators at the department of corrections softball game, they will do so. Contacts make impressions and are remembered and therefore influence the formal process. Cloakroom politics is characterized by debate, discussion, compromise, and appeals for relief. When power is fragmented, as it is in most state assemblies, and certainly congress, a number of personal contacts with representatives can be more fruitful than arguments in front of a subcommittee.

Van Horn also discussed the importance of executive politics. Chief executives—appointed, elected, or upper-level careerists in public agencies—have the advantage of visibility and credibility. Their thoughts, ideas, and values are held in esteem. Their experience level is high and they have made a great deal of contacts while moving up the hierarchical ladder. Therefore, when legislators or the department heads are adamant about the negative outcomes of privatization of prisons, or when they voice suspicions or express lack of knowledge, other actors (especially those not too familiar with corrections) lend these leaders' statements a high amount of legitimacy and credibility. Chief executives build and dominate the government agenda. If contracting for services, especially correction services, which are a large budget item everywhere, means changing the power structure or decreasing agency turf, might that not factor into the chief executive's willingness (or unwillingness) to support the movement? Crisis policy is nearly always centralized through the executive where other policy-making may have other actors involved. Isn't corrections in a state of crisis? Aren't most states unable to resolve their prison overcrowding problems and budget deficits?

Lastly, Van Horn introduces the notion of living room politics. This is the creation and influencing of public opinion and how public opinion in turn influences policy-making. Information "gatekeepers" such as editors, media owners, and journalists are the door through which political information flows. Their perceptions and values tailor information significantly. The general public develops opinion only from information to which it has access. If the media distorts an issue or fails to report on it fully, the public is affected directly. This eventually translates into misinformed representatives in local and state legislative bodies. Living room politics is the expression of opinion by a majority of constituents about particular issues. Unless a crisis causes the public to rise up, arguments over ideology or rationality fall upon deaf legislative ears. As the public is not particularly interested in or aware of the privatization movement, legislators and executives spend their limited time and effort on other matters.

Responses to Survey Regarding Policy-making

During the survey and interview process of the comparison of private and public prisons, many questions were asked private and public managers and their staffs about their perceptions regarding policy-making in general and certain aspects of policy-making in particular. The remainder of this chapter is a discussion about those questions and their responses.

Private managers were asked whether they would able to meet the need for increased cell space quickly. Yes, was the overall response. Not only will lack of red tape allow companies to build or add-on quickly, but capital can be amassed easily, without referenda or tax measures being debated and put to a vote. "Private companies are in the ball game of improvement. They do it every day," said a private operator. Some claimed a year or more advantage. Public managers agreed with the private managers' assessment.

A second question was whether state or federal authorities should delegate authority to manage prisons to the private sector. Private and public managers agreed that enabling legislation is crucial. Legislators lend credibility to the movement if they debate and pass laws supporting prison privatization. Local governments are less reluctant to buy into the process when the issue has the approval of the legislature. The U.S. Constitution does not disallow private prisons and most state constitutions provide for a bidding and contract process. Some believe that private sector involvement is necessary as a check and balance against public sector waste and malfeasance. Public managers agreed here also, though one felt that prisoners are a "ward of the state" and therefore should only be relegated to state control, regardless.

Private managers were asked about liability claims and who would be responsible. They felt that the private company can shield the state through insurance against most medical and physical risks but the state would certainly remain ultimately responsible for claims of unconstitutional treatment and abridgment of individual rights. The private managers believe that because the prison is run according to state standards (cell space per prisoner, for instance), unless the contractor changes the standards their responsibility is to meet them, not be responsible for their constitutionality.

When asked if they thought police power should be delegated to private company managers, private managers pointed out that it already is. They reported that half the police in the United States are private policemen. The Constitution does not disallow it (in fact the first militia mentioned in the Second Amendment consisted of farmers and private citizens who owned guns). Private managers argue that the burden is on government to prove why private police should *not* be allowed to carry arms, given proper training and testing. One of the private prisons contracted with the local police union to provide prison guards. There is a case of a city contracting with a private company who in turn contracts with public-sector policemen to work as civilian employees carrying guns. The point made by private managers is that as long as the training and requirements of prison guards is the same in either sector, then why should privately-employed guards not be responsible to use force, and not allowed to carry weapons?

Every public manager thought this argument was absurd. Guards are an arm of the state and only the state has the right to take life—the extreme case in point. The private managers believe that the only difference between private and public guards is the source that pays them.

Private managers were asked if they thought prisoners in their facilities receive better or different justice than prisoners located in the public jails. The consensus was that justice is given out by the court and that a prison—public or private—merely carries out the order of holding the convict. However, if justice is thought of as a function of treatment while in prison, because private prisons must meet contract requirements or lose the contract, they are actually under more pressure to ensure good treatment according to the requirements of that contract.

Managers were asked if they thought that private sector could do any better at arranging prison space for special prisoners such as AIDS carriers, handicapped, or mentally ill prisoners. Private managers believed private companies to be more flexible and more able to implement innovation and new treatments without bidding procedures, testing requirements, or lengthy and complicated procurement measures (Chi 1989, 74). Public managers believed individuals with special needs would be too costly and that private prisons would want to skim the "cream" of the least-cost prisoners, leaving the state with the burden of difficult prisoners. In response, private managers pointed out that whoever the contract states is to be housed and managed, that is who they will take into the facility. No prisoner is any less dangerous, or to be treated more leniently, than another. They all need bars, guards, and food. Other costs of special care is minimal comparatively and would be an extra cost for either sector.

Can government ensure against private companies underbidding the contract (low balling) in order to get on board and then later raise the price or require more money once they are locked in? Private managers again look to the contract as the best mechanism to relieve governments of that risk and uncertainty. Contracts can be given for long terms, to decrease the low-balling affect, or can be given frequently to engender competition. One manager suggested that if government can't control a contract, why are they managing prisons?

Prison managers were asked about the possibility of prisons

becoming "factories within fences," as suggested by Justice Warren Burger in the 1970s. Public managers were quick to point out the illegality in most states of prisons producing goods that would compete on the "open" market. Private managers suggested that since most prison companies had parent firms, they could more easily acquire raw materials and link production to a market because they already are in the marketplace and are bottom-line oriented. Managers believed it would be better if prisoners worked at other than in-house chores. Work-release only affects about 5 per cent of the prisoners. An in-house factory could provide rehabilitation skills to prisoners, even high-risk prisoners who are not eligible for work-release. Public managers voice the concern that even if it were legal, the introduction of the "make-'em-work" concept would bring with it the making of weapons, dealing in contraband, and a reluctance by many to work. The system would then be bogged down with an investment that would not pay off and would eventually be abandoned, costing taxpayers more money.

Some final general comments by the private managers are of interest. Regarding rehabilitation, private managers felt that if America treats prison as a government-run monopoly, it does an injustice to the prisoners and the economy. Prisoners do not have the advantage of a wide range of management styles and support mechanisms, decreasing the likelihood of change occurring to a broken-down rehabilitation system. Private companies are kept from competing among themselves and with government, relieving the public sector from having to be as efficient and effective in managing prisons.

Private managers believe that special pressure groups and government do not want prisons privatized. Public unions, fearful of change or job loss, undermine the production of legislation enabling prison change. Also, legislatures are unwilling to take the risk to at least support privatization on some small scale because of fear of voter backlash should a company fail or problems occur. At the local level, corrections commissions stand to lose direct control over institutions. Power loss is an anathema to public officials used to guaranteed administrative jurisdictions or wielding power over large budgets.

Private managers believe that unwillingness to allow the movement to grow stems from the fear the private company managers and employees would not be competent in carrying out their responsibilities or that undesirable or neglectful practices might become the norm. They are quick to point out, however, that private companies work in an open setting, are under public scrutiny all the time, and are continually barraged with requests by interested parties who want to visit the prisons and discuss operations and philosophy. The more prisons that go private, the greater the number of requests to visit, look at, and analyze their operations. Any inappropriate practices, decline in the quality of services or malfeasance would surely be detected and the movement would prove itself useful or worthless.

Private companies believe that policy-making for private prisons will continue to be stalled or subverted as long as policy-making is based on tradition and incrementalism rather than efficiency, productivity, and rationality. Policymakers' perceptions of administrators (civilians) running prisons is one of men in ties carrying rifles, not knowing what end to point at who. Policymakers will need to face the question of whether to privatize by considering the relevant facts and past record of the bidding companies when making rational-comprehensive decisions about privately-managed prisons (Nigro and Nigro 1989). Other values, ideals, beliefs, and fears cloud the issue, modify reality, and result in improper choices.

In the final chapter of this book, important questions about prison privatization are revisited and conclusions are restated in more detail. The importance of standards and contracts is discussed as well as the future of the privatization of prisons movement.

6

Future of Private Prisons

This chapter will re-examine the research conclusions relative to the original goals of this study. It will also be determined whether an effort should be made by the public sector toward increasing contracting with private companies for the operation and management of entire correctional facilities.

Goals Revisited

The first goal of this study was to determine whether the privatization of correctional facilities is a viable option for the future of institutional corrections. Three important considerations have been identified. First, private facility operators all indicated that in order to contract for the operation of other correctional facilities, they will be seeking out states and jurisdictions that look favorably upon privatization in general and the privatization of prisons and jails specifically. Several states already have, in the last five years, enacted enabling legislations to help foster the growth of private sector operation of correctional facilities (Durham 1986, 1477–78). Without enabling legislation, private companies are hesitant to risk their efforts trying to establish a new industry, only to be met, down the road, with inordinate opposition or a moratorium as was the case in Pennsylvania (Hornblum 1985, 25–29). Enabling legislation can better reflect a state's intention of support for the idea of prison privatization and its willingness to participate in the movement. As more states enact supportive legislation, the future of prison privatization will become an optimistic one.

Another consideration for future private prison planning is cost-efficiency. As government continues to grow and deficit spending continues to inflate the entire cumulative deficit, governments at all levels will be looking even more closely at viable ways to reduce spending. The three private facilities visited were operated at lower costs per inmate than the three public facilities visited. In addition, each private facility had more programs available than its public counterpart. Also, the overall condition of two of the three private facilities was notably better than the condition of the comparable public facilities. These observations may be a result of the fact that public prison facilities do not operate with private motives and incentives and hence operate less efficiently. Or, these observations may be the result to some phenomenon like the Hawthorne Effect, where, because the population of private prisons is so small, every prison tends to operate at peak efficiency as a result of outside observers evaluating and monitoring their operations (Katz and Kahn 1978, 28). The fact remains that the private prison operators of this study are operating more efficiently than the public operators. This fact supports the argument that government should take a more serious look at private prisons as an alternative to public "production" of correctional services.

A third consideration planners may have for the future of private prisons has to do with contracts and standards. Without the up-front specificity of clear contract requirements and the guidance of agreed-upon standards, a great deal of uncertainty will exist in the private prison industry. The higher the level of uncertainty, the more limited the participation by vendors or governments in contracting out for prison operations. Properly negotiated contracts can shield a government contractor from much of the monetary aspects of liability and the direct costs of litigation by requiring the private operator to hold the government harmless for cases in which monetary liability is found or in which attorneys fees are awarded (Collins 1987, 28). Thus, a hold harmless provision and an insurance requirement clause within a contract might shift some of the burden of liability claims away from the contracting government. William Collins has said, "If a privately [operated] corrections facility can be operated better than a government [operated] facility, the number of losing liability cases should decrease" (Collins 1987, 28).

Private prisons, because of liability costs, have a more immediate reason to reduce litigation where public operated prisons do not. The standards to which the contracted operator will be held accountable, whether to those of the American Corrections Association Commission on Accreditation, state developed standards, or others, must be well defined in the contract (Mullen, Chotabor, and Carrow 1985, 78). In addition to well-defined standards, aggressive contract monitoring by the public agency is critical to the success of the contractual relationship. Other contract provisions essential to a strong relationship between government and vendor that were identified during on-site visits include: problem adjudication procedures, precise sanctions, training requirements, failure option (bankruptcy, disaster, et cetera), defined relationships with the law enforcement community, duration, payment provisions, minimum and maximum occupancy levels, and types of inmates to be detained (Collins 1987; Mullen, Chotabor, and Carrow 1985; Wecht 1987). It must be remembered too, that contract monitoring is essential if a clear and comprehensive contract is to remain a reliable, viable tool for ensuring production and effectiveness. John Rehfuss states, "Any serious analysis of contract monitoring eventually focuses on three major concerns. These issues are the frequently high cost of monitoring, the techniques involved in monitoring and who should perform the monitoring" (Rehfuss 1990; Durham 1988).

With the proper contracts, standards, supportive legislation, and the efficient operational techniques of private enterprise, the future of prison privatization could be one of growth and competition with the publicly operated facilities. Charles Logan points out that there may be a conflict between the "rigidity" of a contract and a private firm's ability to be innovative, and hence, efficient.

> Contracts produce their own form of rigidity, and it will be harder for the government, under contracting, to order and control marginal changes. As two sociologists put it: 'How can innovation be expected from a contractor who will not offer one iota more than the contract calls for and who does not have even the limited flexibility of the state and national correctional programs?' This all-or-nothing reasoning, however, is clearly a false dilemma. Private prisons can have latitude in some respects without being given free rein in all respects. (Logan 1990, 163)

The second goal of this study was to determine whether private companies could manage prisons more efficiently than public operators. In other words, are private companies able to provide the same level of cell space and programs for the same or less cost to taxpayers? First, prompting this study was the absence of empirical data on the costs of commercial prisons (Logan and Rausch 1985, 310). As discussed earlier, an attempt was made by the National Institute of Justice (NIJ) through the Camp and Camp study performed in 1984 to determine the extent to which public correctional facilities issued contracts to the private sector for the production of services such as laundry, food, health, and so on, within publicly-operated facilities (Camp and Camp 1984). Given the extensive and growing use of contracting for prison services as documented by the Camp and Camp survey, it was clear that public prison officials and correction administrators believe that it is cheaper for them to farm out various aspects of corrections. As

Charles Logan states, this "may not prove, but certainly does suggest, that it could also be cheaper to administer an entire subsystem, such as a prison, under private contract" (Logan and Rausch 1985, 310). A review of the data collected during on-site evaluations and review of contracts of the three private and three public prison facilities of this study, reveals that the three privately-operated facilities are operated at less cost to the taxpayers. The efforts of public prison officials to privatize prison services at an increasing rate (as documented by the Camp and Camp study), the results of this study's comparative cost analysis, and future research, may give greater support to the argument that private operation of prison facilities is as efficient (or more efficient) than public prison operation.

A third goal of this study was to attempt to identify the real (as opposed to perceived) barriers that inhibit the entrance of private companies into the private prison market, as well as barriers that make continued operation of private prisons difficult. There is a significant difference between what public and private prison operators view as important barriers to privatization of prisons. Table 6.1 illustrates the differences and types of issues being claimed as significant barriers in the privatization literature, by public prison officials, and by operators of private prisons.

The one issue claimed by the literature and both sector's operators as a major barrier to privatization of prisons is the high cost or unavailability of liability insurance. Three other issues that the literature and public prison operators attested to as being significant are: the possible decline in the quantity and/or quality or services or programs available to inmates, the probable decline in the quality or level of personnel (especially guards and counselors), and the unconstitutionality of governmental delegation of police powers to private company employees. These three issues were not mentioned at all during any private operator interviews as being significant barriers to private operation of a prison. The question of the constitutionality of delegating police powers was nullified with regard to the Butler County Jail, given that guards remained county employees and were deputized by the county sheriff. Whether this method of bestowing police power on guards, doing so by statute, or by some other method should be used for empowering guards at privately-operated prisons remains to be seen. Non-deputized counselors who are guards at Weaversville and Silverdale regularly use restraint techniques (short of deadly force) to control inmates when necessary. Neither of the three private operations have experienced legal problems or political conflict over this issue from local sources or national interest groups.

Table 6.1
Most Frequent Perceived Barriers To Private Prison Operations
(in declining order of frequency of mention)

According to the Literature	Public Prison Operator Opinions	Private Prison Operator Opinions
High Cost Liability Insurance	High Cost Liability Insurance	High Cost Liability Insurance
Decline in level and quality of services	Decline in level and quality of services	Union opposition
Decline in level and quality of personnel	Decline in level and quality of personnel	Civil Service opposition
Constitutionality of delegating police powers	Constitutionality of delegating police powers	Capital for start-up and building
Circumvention of Democracy	Privates unable to meet rigorous state or ACA standards	Cop to civilian status change
No standards for operations for training personnel	Zoning problems	Local political climate
Constitutionality of delegating the prison function	Union Busting and loss of government control	Perception of "executives" running prisons
Parole, good time, discipline decisions conflict with profit motives		

Compiled from a review of current literature and results of structured interviews with public and private prison officials.

Table 6.1 displays other significant issues mentioned by the literature, by the public operators, and by the private operators. The issues brought forth in current literature deal with larger questions such as prison privatization's impact upon democracy, the constitutionality of delegating prison functions, and standards for prison operation. The three remaining issues presented by public prison officials as significant are issues characteristically problematic of public prison operations such as zoning (building a prison in a new locality), unions, and the meeting of state or national standards.

The six issues noted in table 6.1 that were raised by private prison officials as significant barriers were: national union opposition and lobbying efforts, public prison administrators' opposition, local political climate, perceptions about private managers operating prisons, civil service opposition, and capital availability. The private facilities visited were each able to overcome these barriers with effort, research and an assertive posture taken by the parent companies toward media and national opposition groups.

The Future of Privatization of Correctional Institutions

What, then, are the public sector's motivations for supporting the privatization of jails ad prisons? If the results of this study's evaluations of three privately-operated correctional facilities are to be found representative of the impact of privatization upon the population of jails and prisons, then one motivation to continue the prison privatization movement would be the savings of tax revenues through more efficiently-operated private prisons. As we know, however, two of the three privately-operated facilities studied were county level institutions and one was a juvenile facility. No large state prisons were included in this study as there are not, as yet, any that are privately operated. Evaluation of a privately-operated major prison will have to await that day when a major prison's operations are contracted.

An additional motivation for the public sector to support the prison privatization movement is to spread the cost of liability round. As discussed earlier, private operators have an implicit motivation to defend themselves against liability claims. Governments can gain by writing contracts that hold government harmless against monetary sanctions under certain conditions.

A third motivation to support prison privatization is that by doing so the public sector increases its scope of options and alternatives for doing business and also allows the criminal justice system to evaluate itself through comparative analyses and ongoing monitoring. In addition, new techniques developed by private prison operators could be shifted to the public prison operations. Proven standards and methods used by the public prisons can be shifted to the private prisons. There is the possibility that the parent organizations of private prison companies will bring to the prisons the benefit of innovations, new ideas and techniques that will allow prisoner rehabilitation to once again be a reality and not just a dream (Geis 1987; Robbins 1986;

Dunham 1986). Eventually, Justice Burger's vision of prisons as "factories within fences" could become a reality (Hennessey 1986, 10). In the United States there are approximately 750,000 criminals in detention on any given day. This body of people can continue to exist in idleness in the current system or the public sector can risk the status quo for the possible benefits that a growing privatization of prisons movement might bring.

Appendix: Site Review Questionnaire

Facility Name: Class Inmates:
Contractor: Date in Operation:
Occupancy   Security Level:
Capacity:

Specific Questions

1. Cost of Operating 2 years and 1 year before takeover?
   Who to contact?
2. Public access (press, public officials, civilians)?
3. Local opposition? Zoning problems? Before start-up? Now?
4. It is argued that private operators have more flexibility with the use of manpower (hire, fire, reorganize). Comments?
   Union problems?
   Morale problems?
   Personnel costs lower? Why?
   How many employees? Organization Chart?
   Employee benefits: less, more, same?
   Employee training: less, more, same?
5. What are your contingency plans for:
   strike
   bankruptcy
   emergency disasters
   Back-up locations?
   Who takes over
6. It is argued that private companies, by nature, are more efficient. Comment.
   Best cost-saving measure?
   Second best cost-saving measure?
   Have county/state costs declined due to privatization?
   What percentage?
7. Do you have better accountability and record-keeping than private (public) prisons?
8. Who monitors the operation of this prison?
   How?
   Who incurs the costs?
   Different in private (public) facility?

9. How do you treat the trade-off between the need to provide the inmates needs so to comply with the constitution (fifth and fourteenth amendments of due process and eighth amendment of cruel and unusual punishment) and the need to be cost effective?
10. Who performs discipline hearings? How are good time decisions made? Parole decisions?
11. Prison rules: How detailed are they? Any complaints from interest groups? Prisoners?

Programs

1. What programs and benefits are provided to inmates?
    Fill out form!
2. What prominent environmental/local factors impact on this operation to make it more efficient or more costly than it would otherwise be?
3. Health programs:
    what consists of:
    monthly usage rates:
    number of staff, kind of staff:
    goals and objectives (written policies and goals):
    quality assurance methods:
4. Education programs:
    what consists of:
    monthly usage rate:
    number of staff:
    goals and objectives (written policies and goals):
    quality assurance methods:

Barriers

1. The four main barriers to private companies entering the private prison market are: (comment in detail and how was barrier overcome?)
    — Public concern over treatment, level and quality of prison life.
    — Cost of liability insurance.
    — Circumvention of public referendum.
    — No formal standards/guidelines exist for operating prisons. No standards for training guards?
2. What, in your opinion, are the real barriers to entering the prison market?
3. What is inhibiting the growth of the private prison industry?
4. Can private companies provide cell space and prison management at less cost than public?
5. Why should privatization of prisons be perpetuated?

General Questions

1. Are private operators able to provide/raise more cell space quicker than public operators? why?

2. Should the state be able to delegate the operation of a prison/detention center to a private company? comments?
3. What about liability for claims? who is responsible? State of private operator or no one?
4. Can/should police power be delegated to private company?
   How formally done at your facility?
   How many guards do you have?
   Do they carry weapons?
   Incidence of use of weapons (last 12 months).
5. How does privatization ensure better justice for society with regard to prisoners and sentencing?
6. Are private operators better able to provide specialized prisons for groups such as: AIDS carriers, handicapped, mentally ill, protective custody? Why?
7. What do you think about lease-purchase financing?
   Financing from tax revenues?
   Bond issuance financing?
8. It is believed that free market companies tend to become oligopolies or monopolies; hence costs rise. Do you see this as a possibility with the private prison industry?
9. How can government insure against underbidding by private companies in order to gain the contract?
10. It has been said that private prison operators will try to "skim the cream" and seek to house lowest cost, least problem, inmates. Comment!
11. Can private companies use political influence to benefit prisons/prisoners?
12. Are private prisons better able to become "factories within fences" (Justice Burger) than public prisons? How? Why?
13. Prison businesses may eventually lobby for longer sentences or advertise in attempt to influence public opinion about crime — in order to result in longer sentences. Comment?
   Advertise to redirect social policy through fear?
14. It is argued that privatization of prisons will circumvent democracy (ie. no referenda). Comment.
15. How can the contracting government ensure against abuse and unfair treatment when they are not on premises at all times?
16. How can contractors ensure against graft or corruption?
17. AFGE President David Kelly states that lower costs (private operations) will mean less personnel, escapes, inhumane treatment and less personnel? Comment?

Checklist of programs in your facilities.

Program	Have	Do Not Have
A Community treatment center		
B Food service contracted		
C Security services contracted		

Program	Have	Do Not Have
D Transportation		
E Vocational programs		
F Educational programs		
G Video programming		
H Religious programs		
I Aftercare		
J Drug treatment		
K Mental health		
L Health services		
M Blood Bank		
N Private usage of inmate labor		
O College programs		
P cultural programs		
Q Inmate Businesses		
R Work release		
S Training for staff		
T Therapeutic training of inmates		
U Computer services		
V Drama, dancing, etc		
W Canteen, commissary		
X Physicians, nutritionists		
Y Hobbycrafts		
Z Recreation Therapy		
AA Sec offender therapy		
BB Laundry		
CC Maintenance		
DD Personnel or placement services		
EE Counselling		
FF Others not listed		

Notes

Chapter 1. Privatization Overview

1. Information was drawn from Stuart M. Butler, *Privatizing Federal Spending* (New York: Universe Books, 1985), p. 6; *The Budget of the United States*, Fiscal Year 1992, Historical Tables (Washington, D.C.: U.S. Government Printing Office, 1991).

2. Information was drawn from *The Budget of the United States*, ibid.

3. See U.S. Congress, Joint Economic Committee on Monetary and Fiscal Policy, *Privatization of the Federal Government*, Hearings, Ninety-Eighth Congress, 1, 2, and 30 May 1984.

Chapter 2. Privatization: History and Commitment in the United States

1. Quote can be found in both Woodrow Wilson's article "The New Meaning of Government," *Woman's Home Companion* 39, no. 11 (November 1912); and Charles T. Goodsell's, "The Grace Commission: Seeking Efficiency For the Whole People?" *Public Administration Review* 44 (May/June 1984): 196.

2. This table was borrowed from Will Myers, "Proposition 13: Nationwide Implications," *National Tax Journal* 32 (1979): 172.

3. See the introduction to Office of Management and Budget, *Enhancing Governmental Productivity Through Competition: A Progress Report on OMB Circular No. A-76* (Washington: Government Printing Office, March 1984).

4. This is a generalization put forth by the following authors: Abramovitz 1986; Peterson 1986; Bennett and Johnson 1980; Schlesinger 1986; and Leat 1986.

5. This and other useful tables to understand delivery methods can be found in Harry P. Hatry, *Private Approaches for Delivery of Public Services* (Washington, D.C.: Urban Institute Press, 1983), chapter 1.

Chapter 3. The Prison Privatization Movement

1. See Calvert R. Dodge, *A Nation Without Prisons* (Lexington, Mass.: Lexington Books, 1975), p. 3. Also, author's discussions with staff members of the New Jersey Department of Corrections.

2. For a detailed discussion of the case of *Wolf* v. *McDonnell*, 1974, see Robert

116 NOTES

M. Carter, Daniel Glaser, and Leslie T. Wilkens, *Correctional Institutions*, third edition (Cambridge, Mass.: Harper and Row Publishers, 1985), p. 101.

3. Support for this statement can be found in DiPaola 1986; Travis 1985; Krajick 1984; Fenton 1985; Cullen 1986; Fixler 1984; and Logan 1985.

4. See U.S. Congress, House, Committee on the Judiciary, Subcommittee on Courts, Civil Liberties, and Administration of Justice, *Privatization of Corrections*, Hearing, Ninety-ninth Congress, 13 November, 1985 and 18 March, 1986; also Travisono 1984; Jayewardene and Talbot 1982; Swart 1982; Fox 1977; and Tappan 1951.

5. See Gilbert Geis, "Privatization of Prisons: Panacea or Placebo?," in Barry J. Carroll, et al., *Private Means To Public Ends* (New York: Praeger Co., 1987), p. 94. See also, Ira P. Robbins, "Privatization of Corrections," *Judicature* 69 (April/May, 1986), p. 331. Also, Patrick Anderson, et al., "Private Corporations: Feast or Fiasco," *Prison Journal* 65 (Autumn/Winter 1985): 3–4.

6. For further discussion, see Dunham 1986, 1498. See also Geis 1987, 94; Hornblum 1985, 25; Council of State Governments (CSG) 1985; Mullen, Chotabor, and Carrow, 1985; Patrick 1986, 68; and Cullen 1986, 8–16.

7. Information was obtained during on-site visits at Butler County Prison and Hamilton County Prison; 4 and 15 September, 1987.

8. See Dunham 1986, 1477–78 n. 20. Also, "Privatization in Pennsylvania Prison System," 1985; U.S. Congress House Committee on the Judiciary, Subcommittee on Courts, Civil Liberties, and Administration of Justice 1986, Norman A. Carlson's testimony.

9. Gilbert Geis, 1987, 90 [Civil Actions No. 4–81–2928 and 3242 (Houston, Texas: Southern District of Texas) U.S. District Court]. Also, Ira P. Robbins, 1986 (see n. 16).

10. See Robbins, 1986, 328 n. 19. Also see notes 25 and 30.

11. Robbins 1986 [Sinnot v. Davenport, 63 U.S. 227, 243 (1959).]

12. Mayer 1986; *Rendell-Baker* v. *Kohn*, 457 U.S. 830, 843, 102 S.Ct. 2764, 2772 (1982).

13. Charles Logan (1990, 188) developed a typology of ways a private firm might reduce liability risks. Some elements include:
(1) Running prisons better, and thus avoiding lawsuits.
(2) Achieving certification, which greatly enhances the defense against lawsuits.
(3) Carrying adequate and cost-effective insurance.
(4) Agreements in which the contractor defends the government in court and indemnifies it against legal damages.
(5) Developing extensive legal expertise and resources, both for preventing and for fighting lawsuits.
(6) Settling quickly out of court, which is easier for private firms than for public entities.

14. See also U.S. Congress 1986; Donahue 1989, 155.

15. See Geis 1987; Cullen 1986; Patrick 1986; Mullen 1985; Council of State Governments 1986; Hornblum 1985; and Dunham 1986.

16. Information for table and figure collected during research and literature review. Table information was updated via telephone exchanges nad correspondence with principles such as: INS's Bob Schmidt, 8 August, 1987, telephone discussions; U.S. Marshall's Service's James Wilmer, 25 August, 1987, telephone discussions; Florida Dept. of Health and Rehab. Services's Judy Haynes, 10 August 1987, telephone discussion; Texas Dept. of Corrections' Bill Burke, 25 August, 1987, telephone discussions; Colo. Dept. of Criminal Justice's Kurt Gatlin, 25 August, 1987, telephone discussion and further readings done in 1991.

Chapter 4. Comparison of Private and Public Prison Programs, Costs, and Facilities

1. These sources were tapped to uncover prison locations: Pennsylvania Department of Welfare, Jack Godlesky, 5 August, 1987, and New Jersey Department of Corrections, Lou Scavo and David Harris, 21 August, 1987 and 17 September, 1987.

2. Comparison criteria was chosen with the help of experts from the New Jersey Department of Corrections, Professors from the Criminal Justice and Political Science Departments of Trenton State College and criteria discussed in Hatry, et al., 1979.

3. The questionnaire was developed using some of the information located in Camp and Camp, 1984, and Mullen, 1985.

4. Data and information for the study of the Weaversvaille Intensive Treatment Unit were gathered on 3 September, 1987, including interviews with Director Henry Gursky and other staff members.

5. Data and information for the study of the North Central Intensive Treatment Unit were gathered on 28 September, 1987, including interviews with Director Dick Kelley and other staff members.

6. Pennsylvania State Department of Public Welfare, Children, Youth and Families Bulletin (Harrisburg, Pa.: Department of Public Welfare, 30 April, 1987, 14 November, 1986, and 15 November, 1985).

7. Ibid.

8. Data and information for the study of the Butler County Jail were gathered on 4 September, 1987, including interviews with the Administrative Assistant Gweneth Nash and other personnel.

9. Data and information for the study of the Salem County Jail were gathered on 5 October, 1987, including interviews with James Hefner and other personnel.

10. Data and information for the study of the Silverdale Correctional Center were gathered on 13 and 14 September, 1987, including interviews with Director Charles Blanchette, Assistant John Abuso, and other personnel.

11. Data and information for the study of the Warren County Correctional Center were gathered on 6 October, 1987, including interviews with Director Robert Sharr and other personnel.

12. Issues to be evaluated regarding the privatization of prisons were identified during on-site visits, discussions with officials from the New Jersey and Pennsylvania Departments of Corrections, officials from the Pennsylvania Departments of Welfare, colleagues at Temple University and Trenton State College, and all the available literature on the subject.

References

ABA Urges Moratorium on Prison/Jail Privatization. 1986. *Corrections Digest* 17: 6–7.

Abromvitz, M. 1986. The Privatization of the Welfare State. *Social Work* 31: 257–64.

AFSCME. 1984. *Passing The Bucks*. Washington, D.C.: AFL-CIO.

Anderson, James E. 1984. *Public Policymaking: An Introduction*. Boston: Houghton-Mifflin Co.

Anderson, Patrick, Charles R. Davoli, and Laura J. Moriarity. 1985. Private Corrections: Feast or Fiasco. *Prison Journal* 65 (Fall/Winter).

Auerbach, Barbara. 1972. The Private Sector Re-enters the Field. *Prison Journal* 52: 25–36.

Bacas, Harry. 1984. When Prisons and Profits Go Together. *Nations's Business* (October): 62–63.

Barnes, Harry E. 1974. *Criminal Justice in America*. New York: Arno Press.

Becker, Craig, and Amy Dru Stanley. 1985. The Down-side of Private Prisons. *The Nation* (June 15): 235–37.

Bennett, Georgett. 1987. *Crime Warps*. New York: Doubleday and Co.

Bennett, James T., and Manuel H. Johnson. 1980. Tax Private Sector Production of Public Service. *Public Finance Quarterly* 8: 363–96.

———. 1979. Public vs. Private Provision of Collective Goods and Services: Garbage Collection Revisited. *Public Choice* 34: 55–63.

Berger, Peter L., and Richard J. Neuhaus. 1977. *To Empower People*. Washington, D.C.: American Enterprise Institute.

Bivens, Terry. 1986. Can Prisons For Profit Work? *The Philadelphia Inquirer Magazine* (August 3): 14–25.

Blakely, Steve. 1986. Officials Say Budget Hits States, Cities the Hardest. *Congressional Quarterly Weekly Report* 44 (February 15): 309–11.

Bowsher, Charles A. 1986. Federal Cutbacks Strengthen State Role. *State Government News* 29, no. 2 (February): 18–22.

Break, George F. 1979. Interpreting Proposition 13: A Comment. *National Tax Journal* 32 (June): 43–50.

Breaking Up Government's Monopoly On Prison Cells. *New York Times* (March 3), 22E.

Buchanan, James A., and Richard E. Wagner. 1967. *Public Debt in a Democratic Society*. Washington, D.C.: American Enterprise Institute.

Buchanan, James A. 1968. *The Demand and Supply of Public Goods*. Chicago: Rand McNally and Company.

Burright, David. 1990. Privatization of Prisons: Fad or Future? *FBI Law Enforcement Bulletin* (February): 1–4.

Butler, Stuart. 1985. *Privatizing Federal Spending*. New York: Universe Books.

_____. 1984. The Privatization Option: A Strategy of Shrinking the Size of Government. Washington, D.C.: Heritage Foundation.

Caldwell, Lynton K. 1944. *The Administrative Theories of Hamilton and Jefferson*. Chicago: University of Chicago Press.

Camp, Camile G., and George M. Camp. 1985. *The Real Cost of Corrections*. New York: Criminal Justice Institute.

_____. 1984. *Private Sector Involvement in Prison Services and Operations*. Washington, D.C.: National Institute of Corrections, U.S. Department of Justice.

Carlson, Norman A. 1986. Prison Privatization. *Corrections Digest* 17, no. 7: 1–5.

Carroll, Barry J., Ralph W. Conant, and Thomas A. Easton. 1987. *Private Means Public Ends*. New York: Praeger.

Carter, Robert M., Daniel Glazer, and Leslie T. Wilkins. 1985. *Correctional Institutions*. 3rd edition. Cambridge, Mass.: Harper and Row Publishers.

Cebula, Richard J., and Linda Chevlin. 1981. Proposition 4, The Tax Mirage. *American Journal of Economics and Sociology* 40 (October): 343–48.

Chi, Keon S. 1989. Prison Overcrowding and Privatization: Models and Opportunities. *The Journal of State Government* 62: 70–76.

_____. 1985. Privatization: A Public Option?. *State Government News* 27/28 (June): 4–9.

Cikens, Warren I. 1986. Privatization of the American Prison System: An Idea Whose Time Has Come. *Notre Dame Journal of Law, Ethics and Public Policy* 2 (Winter): 445–65.

Clear, Todd R., and George R. Cole. 1986. *Corrections*. Monterey, Calif.: Brooks/Cole Publishing Co.

Clendinen, Dudley. 1985. Officials of Counties Debate Private Jail Operation. *New York Times* (November 4), A27.

Coffey, Alan R. 1975. *Correctional Administration*. Englewood Cliffs, N.J.: Prentice-Hall.

Collins, William. 1987. Privatization: Some Legal Considerations From a Neutral Perspective. *American Jails* (Summer): 28–34.

Conte, Christopher. 1978. Proposition 13 Fallout: Congress Weighs The Message. *Congressional Quarterly Weekly Report* 36 (July 8): 1724–28.

Cook, Brian J., and Stephen L. Elkin. 1985. The Public Life of Economic Incentives. *Policy Studies Journal* 13 (June): 797–813.

Cook, Thomas J., and Frank P. Scioli, Jr. 1972. A Research Strategy for Analyzing the Impact of Public Policy. *Administrative Science Quarterly* 17 (September): 328–39.

Council of State Governments. 1985. Private Jails. Contracting Out Public Service. *CSG Backgrounder* (March): 1–4.

County Sheriffs of Colorado. 1986. Privatization of Correctional Facilities. Position paper prepared in Denver, Colorado, 30 September.

Courant, Paul N. 1980. Why Voters Support Tax Limitation Amendments: The Michigan Case. *National Tax Journal* 33: 1–20.

Cullen, Francis T. 1986. The Privatization of Treatment: Prison Reform in the 1980's. *Federal Probation* 50: 8–16.

DeGeorge, Gail. 1990. Wackenhut Is Out To Prove That Crime Does Pay. *Business Week* (17 December): 95–96.

DiIulio, John J., Jr. 1988. What's Wrong With Private Prisons. *Public Interest*, no. 92 (Summer): 66–83.

_____. 1987. *Governing Prisons*. New York: The Free Press. DiPaolo, Joseph R. 1986. Private Sector-Breaking the Shackles of Tradition. *Corrections Today* 48 (April): 144–46.

Dodge, Calvert R. 1979. *A World Without Prisons*. Lexington, Mass.: Lexington Books.

_____. 1975. *A Nation Without Prisons*. Lexington, Mass.: Lexington Books.

Doig, Jameson. 1983. *Criminal Corrections, Ideals and Realities*. Lexington, Mass.: Lexington Books.

Donahue, John D. 1989. *The Privatization Decision*. New York: Basic Books.

Downs, Anthony. 1984. Alternative Approaches to Coping With a Squeeze on Public Activities. In U.S. Congress, Senate, Committee on Government Affairs. *Alternative Service Delivery, Part 1*. Hearing, 97th Congress, 1st Session.

_____. 1957. *An Economic Theory of Democracy*. New York: Harper and Row.

Drucker, Peter F. 1969. *The Age of Discontinuity*. New York: Harper and Row.

Dunham, Douglas W. 1986. Inmates Rights and the Privatization of Prisons. *Columbia Law Review* 86 (November): 1476–1504.

Dunleavy, Patrick. 1986. Explaining the Privatization Boom: Public Choice Versus Radical Approaches. *Public Administration* 64 (Spring): 13–34.

Durham, Alexis M., III. 1989. Origins of Interest in the Privatization of Punishment: The Nineteenth and Twentieth Century American Experience. *Criminology* 27, no.1: 107–39.

_____. 1988. Evaluating Privatized Correctional Institutions: Obstacles to Effective Assessment. *Federal Probation* (June): 65–71.

Dye, Thomas. 1987. *Understanding Public Policy*. Sixth edition. Englewood Cliffs, N.J.: Prentice-Hall.

Dytianguin, Norman G. 1986. The Economics of Privatization. *C.B. Review* (December): 7–12.

Easton, David, ed. 1965. *A Framework for Political Analysis*. Englewood Cliffs, N.J.: Prentice-Hall.

Elazar, Daniel. 1966. *American Federalism: A View From the States*. New York: Thomas Crowell.

Easton, David. 1957. Approach to the Analysis of Political Systems. *World Politics* 9: 383–400.

Elvin, Jan. 1984. A Civil Liberties View of Private Prisons. *National Prison Project Journal* 1 (Fall): 40–52.

Evans, Brian. 1987. Private Prisons. *Emory Law Journal* 36: 253–83.

Farkas, Gerald M. 1985. Prison Industries. *Corrections Today* (June): 102–3.

Fenton, Joseph. 1985. No Moratorium for Private Prisons. *The Privatization Review* (Fall): 21–24.

Finley, Lawrence K., ed. 1989. *Public Sector Privatization*. New York: Quorum Books.

Finn, Peter. 1984. Judicial Responses to Prison Overcrowding. *Judicature* 67, no. 7: 318–19.

Fitzgerald, Randall. 1988. *When Government Goes Private*. New York: Universe Books.

_____. 1986. Free-Enterprise Jails: Key to Our Prison Dilemma? *Reader's Digest* (March): 85–88.

Fixler, Phillip E. 1984. Behind Bars We Find an Enterprise Zone. *Wall Street Journal* (November): 34.

Floristano, Patricia S., and Stephen B. Gordon. 1980. Public v. Private: Small Government Contracting with the Private Sector. *Public Administration Review* 40 (January/February): 29–43.

_____. 1979. Private Provision of Public Services: Contracting by Large Local governments. *International Journal of Public Administration*, no. 3: 307–27.

Foltz, Kim. 1984. The Corporate Warden. *Newsweek* (May 7).

Fox, Vernon. 1977. *Community-Based Corrections*. Englewood Cliffs, N.J.: Prentice-Hall.

Friedman, Milton. 1962. *Capitalism and Freedom*. Chicago: University of Chicago Press.

_____. 1978. *Tax Limitation, Inflation, and the Role of Government*. Dallas, Texas: Fisher Institute.

Galbraith, John Kenneth. 1952. *American Capitalism*. Boston: Houghton Mifflin Company.

Gallup Organization. 1988. Gallup Poll Results. *Political Index*, no. 337 (September): 20.

Geis, Gilbert. 1987. Privatization of Prisons: Panacea or Placebo? In Carroll, Barry J., et al., eds., *Private Means Public Ends*. New York: Praeger Co.

Gentry, James T. 1986. The Panopticon Revisited. The Problems of Monitoring Private Prisons. *The Yale Law Journal* 96: 353–75.

Gest, Ted. 1984. Prisons For Profit: A Growing Business. *U.S. News and World Report* (July 2): 45–46.

"Getting a Leg Up On Overcrowding." 1986. The Times (Trenton, N.J.) (28 November), A21.

Gilbert, Neil, and Harry Specht, ed. 1979. *Social Services by Government Contract*. New York: Praeger Publishers.

Goodsell, Charles T. 1984. The Grace Commission: Seeking Efficiency for the Whole People?. *Public Administration Review* 44 (May/June) 196–203.

Gordon, George. 1987. *Public Administration In America*. New York: St. Martin's Press.

Hagman, Donald. 1978. Proposition 13: A Prostitution of Conservative Principles. *Tax Review* 39 (September): 39–42.

Hamilton County Government. 1987. Hamilton County Correction Facilities Agreement. Office of the Attorney General, Chattanooga, Tennessee, FY.

Hanke, Steve H., ed. 1987. *Prospects For Privatization*. New York: Academy of Political Science.

_____. 1985. The Theory of Privatization. Paper presented at the Heritage Lectures, Heritage Foundation, Washington, D.C.

Hansen, Marcus L. 1940. *The Atlantic Migration*. London: Oxford University Press.

Harman, Willis W. 1976. *An Incomplete Guide to the Future*. San Franciso: San Francisco Book Co.

Hatry, Harry. 1983. *Private Approaches for Delivery of Public Services*. Washington, D.C.: The Urban Institute.

―――. 1979. *Efficiency Measurement for Local Government Services*. Washington, D.C.: The Urban Institute.

―――. 1976. *Program Analysis for State and Local Governments*. Washington, D.C.: The Urban Institute.

Haveman, Robert H., and Kenyon A. Knopf. 1966. *The Market System*. New York: John Wiley and Sons, Inc.

Haveman, Robert H., and John V. Krutilla. 1968. *Unemployment, Idle Capacity and Evaluation of Public Expenditures*. Baltimore: Johns Hopkins University Press.

Heady, Ferrel. 1984. *Public Administration: A Comparative Perspective*. New York: Market Dekker, Inc.

Heclo, Hugh. 1978. In Anthony King, ed., The New Political System. Washington, D.C.: American Enterprise Institute for Public Policy Research.

Heidenheimer, Arnold J., Hugh Heclo, and Carolyn Teich Adams. 1983. *Comparative Public Policy*. 2nd edition. New York: St. Martin's Press.

Henig, Jeffrey R. 1990. Privatization in the United States: Theory and Practice. *Political Science Quarterly* 104, no. 4: 649-70.

Hennessey, Edward F. 1986. Why Our Jails are Suddenly Overcrowded. *The Judges Journal* 23, no. 1.

High Costs Stir Critics of Privately Operated Jails. *Criminal Justice Newsletter* 16, no. 12 (June 17): 5.

Holsti, Ole R. 1969. *Content Analysis for the Social Science*. Reading, Mass.: Addison-Wesley Publishing Co.

Hood, John. 1990. Kicking the Budget Binge. Paper available from John Locke Foundation, Raleigh, North Carolina, no. 1 (May 2).

Hornblum, Allen. 1985. Are We Ready for Privatization of America's Prisons? *The Privatization Review* (Fall): 25-29.

Hutto, T. Don. 1984. Resigning the Private Correctional Facility. *Corrections Today* 46: 78-79, 85.

Immarigeon, Russ. 1987. Privatizing Adult Imprisonment in the U.S.: A Bibliography. *Criminal Justice Abstracts* (March): 123-39.

Jayewardene, C. H., and C. K. Talbot. 1982. Entrusting Corrections to the Private Sector. *International Journal for Offender Therapy and Comparative Criminology* 26: 177-87.

Jayewardene, C. H., T. J. Juliani, and C. K. Talbot. 1983. Supply Side Corrections or Human Resource Management: A New Strategy for Parole and Probation. *International Journal of Comparative and Applied Criminal Justice* 7, no. 1: 99-108.

Johnson, Judith. 1985. Should Adult Correctional Facilities Be Privately Managed? *National Sheriff* 37 (April & May): 21-23.

Johnson, Paul B. 1990. The Privatization Of Correctional Management: A Review. *Journal of Criminal Justice* 18: 351-58.

_____. 1986. What are the Legal Problems Involved in the Privatization of State/Local Corrections. *Corrections Digest* 17, no. 8: 1–7.

Katz, Daniel and Robert L. Kahn. 1978. *The Social Psychology of Organizations*. New York: John Wiley and Sons.

Kay, J. A., and D. J. Thompson. 1986. Privatization: A Policy in Search of a Rationale. *The Economic Journal* 96 (March): 18–32.

Kelley, Dave. 1986. The Privatization of Corrections. *Corrections Digest* 17 (March 26): 4–6.

King, Wayne. 1984. Contracts For Detention Raise Legal Questions. *New York Times* (March 6), A10.

Klein, Daniel. 1986. Privatization Further Down the Road. *Freeman* 36 (June): 234–35.

Kolderie, Ted. 1986. The Two Different Concepts of Privatization. *Public Administrative Review* (July/August): 285–91.

Krajick, Kevin. 1984. Prisons for Profit: The Private Alternative. *State Legislatures* 10, no. 4 (April): 9–14.

_____. 1984. Punishment for Profit. *Across The Board* 21 (March): 20–27.

_____. 1982. *Overcrowded Time*. New York: McConnel Clark Foundation.

Kroll, Michael A. 1984. Prison for Profit. *Progressive* (September): 18–23.

Ladd, Everette C. 1978. The Tax Revolt. *Public Opinion* 1 (July-August): 29–34.

Ladd, Helen. 1978. An Economic Evaluation of State Limitations on Local Taxing and Spending Powers. *National Journal* 31 (March): 1–19.

Laux, Jeanne Kirk. 1986. Privatization: An International Trend. *International Perspectives* (Canada) (May/June): 7–9.

Lawler, Edward E. 1973. *Motivation In Work Organizations*. Monterey, Calif.: Brooks/Cole Publishing Co.

Leat, Diana. 1986. Privatization and Volunteerism. *Quarterly Journal of Social Affairs* 2, no. 3: 285–320.

Leban, Janet A. 1985. The Pennsylvania Prison Debate. *The Privatization Review* (Fall): 20–21.

Lee, Roger J., and Laurin A. Wollan, Jr. 1985. The Libertarian Prison: Principles of Laissez-Faire Incarceration. *Prison Journal* 65 (Autumn/Winter): 108–21.

Levinson, Robt. B. 1984. Private Sector and Corrections. *Corrections Today* 46 (August): 42, 46.

LeGrand, Julian, and Ray Robinson, eds. 1984. *Privatization and the Welfare State*. London: George, Allen and Unwin.

Levine, Charles. 1986. The Federal government in the Year 2000. *Public Administration Review* 46 (May/June).

_____. 1980. *Managing Fiscal Stress*. Chatham, New Jersey: Chatham House Publishers.

Levine, Charles H., Irene S. Rubin, and George G. Wolohojian. 1981. *The Politics of Retrenchment*. Beverly Hills, Calif.: Sage Publications.

Levinson, Robert B. 1985. *Private Sector Operation of a Correctional Institution*. National Institute of Corrections, U.S. Department of Justice.

Lewis, Orlando F. 1967. *The Development of American Prisons and Prison Customs*. Montclair, N.J.: Patterson Smith.

Light, Richard J., and Paul V. Smith. 1971. Accumulating Evidence: Procedures for Resolving Contradictions Among Different Research Studies. *Harvard Educational Review* 41 (November): 429–71.

Linowes, David. 1989. Privatization For A More Effective Government. *Illinois Business Review* 46: 3–6.

Logan, Charles. 1990. *Private Prisons: Cons and Pros.* New York: Oxford University Press.

_____. 1986. Private Prisons: Part I. *Law Enforcement News* 12:8.

_____. 1985. Competition in the Prison Business. *Freeman* 35: 469–78.

Logan, Charles, and Sharla P. Rausch. 1985. Punish and Profit. *Justice Quarterly* 2, no. 3 (September): 303–18.

Lowery, David. 1982. Interpreting the Tax Revolt: A Review of the Literature and an Alternative Explanation. *State and Local Government Review* 14 (September): 110–16.

Mayer, Connie. 1986. Legal Issues Surrounding Private Operation of Prisons. *Criminal Law Bulletin* 22, no. 4 (July/August): 309–25.

McConnel, Campbell R. 1987. *Economics.* Tenth edition. Hightstown, New Jersey: McGraw-Hill.

McDonald, Douglas, ed. 1990. *Private Prisons and the Public Interest.* New Brunswick, N.J.: Rutgers University Press.

McKelvey, Blake. 1975. *American Prisons.* Montclair, N.J.: Patterson-Smith.

McLaughlin, John. 1986. Going Private. *National Review* (28 February): 24.

Moore, Thomas Gale. 1990. Deregulation, Privatization, and the Market. *National Forum* (Spring): 5–8.

Moore, Stephen. 1987. Contracting Out. In Steve H. Hanke, ed., *Prospects For Privatization.* New York: Academy of Political Science.

Moos, Rudolf H. 1975. *Evaluating Correctional and Community Settings.* New York: John Wiley and Sons.

Moscovitch, Edward. 1985. Proposition 2-1/2: A Worm's Eye View. *Government Finance Review* 1, no. 4 (February): 21–25.

Mullen, Joan. 1985. Corrections and the Private Sector. *The Privatization Review* (Fall): 10–19.

Mullen, Joan, Kent Chotabor, and Deborah Carrow. 1985. *The Privatization of Corrections.* National Institute of Justice. Washington, D.C.: U.S. Department of Justice.

Musgrave, Richard A. 1979. The Tax Revolt. *Social Science Quarterly* 59 (March): 697–703.

Myers, Will. Proposition 13: Nation Wide Implications. *National Tax Journal* 32: 171–75.

Nathan, Richard P. 1985. Reagan and the Cities: How to Meet the Challenge. *Challenge* 28 (September/October): 4–8.

_____. 1983. *The Administrative Presidency.* New York: John Wiley and Sons.

National Institute of Justice. 1985. *The Privatization of Corrections.* Washington, D.C.: Government Printing Press.

National Institute of Law Enforcement and Criminal Justice, Law Enforcement Assistance Administration. 1978. *Contracting For Correctional Services in the Community.* Washington, D.C.: U.S. Government Printing Office.

New Jersey Department of Corrections. 1979. *Manual of Standards for New Jersey Adult County Correctional Facilities*. Trenton, N.J.: Department of Corrections.

Nigro, Felix A., and Lloyd G. Nigro. 1989. *Modern Public Administration*. New York: Harper and Row.

Niskanen. William A. 1979. Tax Limitation In Michigan. *National Tax Journal* 32: 169–71.

Nissen, Theodore. 1985. Free-Market Prisons. *The Nation* (14 September): 194.

Office of Management and Budget. 1987. *Management of the United States Government: Fiscal Year 1986*. Washington, D.C.: Government Printing Office.

_____. 1985. *Supplement — OMB Circular No. A-76 (Revised) Performance of Commercial Activities*. Executive Office of the President. Washington, D.C.: Government Printing Office.

_____. 1984. *Enhancing Governmental Productivity Through Competition: A Progress Report on OMB Circular No. A-76*. Washington, D.C.: Government Printing Press.

_____. 1984. *The Budget In Brief*. Washington, D.C.: Government Printing Office.

Ohashi, Theodore M., and Timothy P. Roth. 1980. *Privatization: Theory and Practice*. Vancouver, B. C., Canada: The Fraser Institute.

Ostrom, Vincent, and Elinor Ostrom. 1977. Public Goods and Public Choices. In E. S. Savas, *Alternatives For Delivery of Public Services*. Boulder, Colo.: Westview Press.

Parker, David. 1990. The 1988 Local Government Act and Compulsory Competitive Tendering. *Urban Studies* 27, no. 5: 653–68.

Patrick, Allen L. 1986. Profit Motive vs. Quality. *Corrections Today* 48 (April): 68, 70, and 74.

Pennsylvania State Department of Public Welfare. 1986. Contract. Department of Welfare and RCA Service Company, 1 November, 1985 to 30 June, 1986. Contract # 805050783.

Pennsylvania State Department of Public Welfare. 1987. Contract. Department of Welfare and RCA Service Company, 1 July, 1986 to 30 June, 1987. Contract # 805060783.

Pennsylvania State Legislature. 1987. *Children, Youth and Families Bulletin*. Harrisburg, Pa.: Department of Welfare (30 April).

_____. 1986. *Children, Youth and Families Bulletin*. Harrisburg, Pa.: Department of Welfare (14 November).

_____. 1985. *Privatization In Pennsylvania Prison System*. Harrisburg, Pa.: State Legislature.

_____. 1985. *Children, Youth and Families Bulletin*. Harrisburg, Pa.: Department of Welfare (15 November).

Peters, Guy B. 1984. *The Politics of Bureaucracy*. 2nd edition. New York: Longman Press.

Peterson, William H. 1986. Privatization: The Rediscovery of Entrepreneurship. *Freeman* 36:312–26.

Pirie, Madsen. 1985. *Dismantling The State*. Dallas, Texas: National Center for Policy Analysis.

Poole, Robert W. Jr. 1984. The Politics of Privatization. In Stuart Butler, *The Privatization Option: A Strategy to Shrink the Size of Government*. Washington: D.C.: Heritage Foundation.

_____. 1982. Rebuilding the Private Sector. *Imprimis* 11:1–6.

_____. 1980. *Cutting Back City Hall*. New York: Universe Books.

President's Private Sector Survey on Cost Control. 1983. *Report on Privatization*. Washington, D.C.: Government Printing Office.

"Proposition 13's Impact." 1982. *Society* 20 (November/December): 7.

Ray, William, and Richard Ravizza. 1985. *Methods*. 2nd. edition. Belmont, California: Wadsworth Publishing Co.

Rehfuss, John. 1990. Contracting Out and Accountability in State and Local Governments—The Importance of Contract Monitoring. *State and Local Government Review* (Winter): 44–48.

"Reagan's Tax Proposals." 1985. *Gallup Report*, no. 238 (July): 14–30.

Ring, Charles. 1987. *Contracting For The Operation of Private Prisons*. College Park, Md.: American Correctional Association.

Robbins, Ira P. 1986. Privatization of Corrections. Judicature 69 (April/May): 325–31.

Roberts, Albert R., and Gerald T. Powers. 1985. The Privatization of Corrections: Methodological Issues and Dilemmas Involved in Evaluative Research. *Prison Journal* 65 (Autumn/Winter): 95–103.

Rose, Richard. 1989. Privatization as a Problem of Satisficing and Dissatisficing. *American Review of Public Administration* 19, no. 2: 98–118.

Rubin, Irene S. 1985. *Shrinking The Federal Government*. New York: Longman Inc.

Ryan, Mick, and Tony Ward. 1989. *Privatization and the Penal System*. New York: St. Martin's Press.

Savas, Emanuel S. 1990. Privatization: A Strategy for Structural Reform. *National Forum* (Spring): 9–11.

_____. 1990. A Taxonomy of Privatization Strategies. *Policy Studies Journal* 18, no. 2: 344–55.

_____. 1987. *Privatization: The Key To Better Government*. Chatham, New Jersey: Chatham House Publishers.

_____. 1984. The Efficiency of the Private Sector. In Stuart Butler, *The Privatization Option: A Strategy to Shrink the Size of Government*. Washington: D.C.: Heritage Foundation.

_____. 1982. *Privatizing The Public Sector*. Chatham, New Jersey: Chatham House Publishers.

_____. 1980. Policy Analysis For Local government. In Charles H. Levine, *Managing Fiscal Stress*. New Jersey: Chatham House.

_____. 1977. Alternatives For Delivery of Public Services. Boulder, Colo.: Westview Press.

Schlesinger, Mark, Robert A. Dorwart, and Richard T. Police. 1986. Purchase of Services. *Journal Of Policy Analysis and Management* 5 (Winter): 245–63.

Sechrest, Dale K., and Ernest G. Reimer. 1982. Adopting National Standards for Correctional Reform. *Federal Probation* (June): 18–25.

Seed, Peter H. 1986. Privatization: An Alternative For Capital-Intensive Public Services. *Minnesota Cities* 71 (January): 4–5.

Seelmeyer, John. 1985. Jails For Profit—A Bad, or Good, Development? *Law and Order* 33 (May): 22–25.

Segarin, Edward. 1986. Private Prisons II. *Law Enforcement News* 12 (May): 8–12.

Seley, John E. and Julian Wolpert. 1985. The Savings/Harm Tableau For Social Impact Assessment of Retrenchment Policies. *Economic Geography* 61 (April): 158–71.

Sellers, Martin P. 1990. Privatization of Urban Services In North Carolina. *Privatization Review* (Summer): 51–64.

———. 1989. Private and Public Prisons: A Comparison of Costs, Programs and Facilities. *International Journal of Offender Therapy and Comparative Criminology* (December): 241–56.

Shick, Allen. 1986. Controlling Non-Conventional Expenditure. *Public Budgeting and Finance* 6 (Spring): 3–19.

Simon, Herbert. 1957. *Administrative Behavior*. New York: Macmillan Press.

Snedeker, Michael. 1986. Private Prisons—A Bankrupt Idea. *The California Prisoner* 15 (November): 5.

Squire, Lyn, and Herman G. VanDerTak. 1975. *Economic Analyses of Projects*. Baltimore: Johns Hopkins University Press.

Stanfield, Rochelle L. 1983. The Taxpayer's Revolt Is Alive Or Dead in the Water— Take Your Pick. *National Journal* 15 (December): 2568–72.

Stanley, David T. 1980. Cities In Trouble. In Charles H. Levine, *Managing Fiscal Stress*. Chatham, New Jersey: Chatham House.

Steelman, D. 1984. *New York City Jail Crises*. New York: The Correctional Association of New York.

Stevens, Barbara. 1984. Comparing Public and Private Sector Privatization Efficiency. *National Productivity Review* (Autumn): table 5.

———. 1984. *Delivering Municipal Services Efficiently*. Washington, D.C.: Department of Housing and Urban Development, Office of Policy Development Research.

Stewart, James. 1985. The Private Sector and Corrections. *Corrections Digest* 16, no. 12 (June): 4–6.

"Still No Rest For Poor Taxpayers". 1984. *U.S. News and World Report* 96 (May 7): 60–61.

Sullivan, Harold J. 1989. Privatization of Corrections and the Constitutional Rights or Prisoners. *Federal Probation* (June): 36–42.

Summers, Anita A. Proposition 13 and Its Aftermath. *Federal Reserve Bank of Philadelphia: Business Review* (March/April): 5–11.

Swart, Stanley L. 1982. Private Sector Corrections in the 1980's/Some Notes. *Journal of Offender Counselling, Services and Rehabilitation* 7 (Fall): 79–82.

Tappan, Paul W., ed. 1951. *Contemporary Correction*. New York: McGraw-Hill.

Tarchys, Daniel. 1985. Curbing Public Expenditures. *Journal of Public Policy* 5 (February): 23–67.

Tax Cut Stampede: Is Washington Panicking? 1980. *U.S. News and World Report* 89 (4 August): 40–41.

Tax Payer Revolt Pays Off. 1978. *U.S. News and World Report* 84 (30 January): 23–24.

Tax Payer Revolt: Where It's Spreading Now. 1978. *U.S. News and World Report* 84 (26 June): 16–19.

Tolchin, Martin. 1986. Bar Group Urges Halt In Use of Privately Run Jails. *New York Times* (February 12), A28.

_____. 1986. Governors' Interest In Private Prisons Rising. *New York Times* (March 2), 35.

_____. 1985. Governors Cautious in Endorsing the Private Operation of Prisons. *New York Times* (March 3), 26.

Travis, Lawrence F., Edward J. Latessa, and Genarro F. Vito. 1985. Private Enterprise and Institutional Corrections. *Federal Probation* 49 (December): 11–16.

Travisono, Anthony P. 1984. A Rose By Any Other Name.... *Corrections Today* 46 (April): 4.

Tuckman, Howard P. 1985. Alternative Approaches To Public Sector Inefficiency. *American Journal of Economics and Sociology* 44 (January): 55–65.

Turnbull, W. N., and A. D. Witte. 1981/1982. Determinants of the Costs of Operating Large Scale Prisons and Implications for the Costs of Correctional Standards. *Law and Society Review* 16, no. 1: 115–34.

U.S. Congress. 1986. *Privatization of Corrections.* Committee on Judiciary, House of Representatives: Subcommittee on Courts, Civil Liberties, and the Administration of Congress. (13 November, 1985 and 18 March, 1986). Washington, D.C.: Government Printing Office.

U.S. Congress. 1985. *Privatization of Prison Construction in New York.* Hearing: Joint Economic Committee of U.S. Congress (5 December).

U.S. Congress. 1984. *Privatization of the Federal Government.* Joint Economic Committee hearings: Subcommittee on Monetary and Fiscal Policy (2, 3, and 30 May).

U.S. Government. 1991. *Budget Of The United States (1992).* Washington, D.C.: U.S. Government Printing Office.

Van Horn, Carl, Donald Bauer, and William Gormley. 1989. *Politics and Public Policy.* Washington, D.C.: CQ Press.

Waldo, Dwight. 1953. *Ideas and Issues in Public Administration.* New York: McGraw-Hill.

Walzer, Michael. 1985. Hold The Justice. *New Republic* (8 April): 10–12.

Warner, Samuel Bass, Jr. 1968. *The Private City.* Philadelphia: University of Pennsylvania Press.

Warren, Robert O. 1966. *Government in Metropolitan Regions: A Reappraisal of Fractionated Political Organization.* University of California, Los Angeles: Institute of Governmental Affairs.

Waste, Robert. 1989. *The Ecology of City Policymaking.* New York: Oxford University Press.

Wayson, B. L., et al. 1981. *Managing Correctional Resources: Economic Analysis Techniques.* Washington, D.C.: U.S. Department of Justice.

Wecht, David N. 1987. Breaking the Code of Deference: Judicial Review of Private Prisons. *Yale Law Journal* 96: 815–37.

Williams, Alan, and Robert Anderson. 1975. *Efficiency in the Social Services.* London: Basil Blackwell.

Wilson, Woodrow. 1912. The New Meaning of Government. *Woman's Home Companion* 39, no. 11 (November).

Wirtzfield, Roy. 1985. New Women's Jail Treats Inmates as Humans. *Law and Order* 33 (May): 23.

Witte, A. D., et al. 1981. *Empirical Investigation of Correctional Cost Functions.* Washington, D.C.: Department of Justice.

Wollan, Laurin A. 1986. Prisons: The Privatization Phenomenon. *Public Administration Review* 46, no. 6 (November/December): 678–81.

Wooley, Mary R. 1985. Prisons For Profit: Policy Considerations For Government Officials. *Dickenson Law Review* 90, no. 2 (Winter): 307–31.

Yin, Robert K., and Karen A. Heald. 1975. Using the Case Survey Method to Analyze Policy Studies. *Administrative Science Quarterly* 20 (September): 371–81.

Index